Answers

JESUS
AND THE
CHRISTIAN
MESSAGE

Preston Condra | Kelly Condra

Answers:
Jesus and the Christian Message
Minnesota-Wisconsin Edition

Resource provided by:
Minnesota-Wisconsin Baptist Convention

By Preston Condra and Kelly Condra
Third Edition et al by Sufficient Word Publishing,
a division of Sufficient Word Ministries, Springdale, AR.
Copyright © 2017 All rights reserved.
Printed in the United States of America.

First Edition by Sufficient Word Publishing. Copyright © 2017
Original Book Title: *I Have Some Good News: The Gospel: Objections and Answers.*
Second Edition by GC2 Press® titled: *Answers: Jesus and the Christian Message.*
Copyright © 2017

No part of this book may be used or reproduced in any manner whatsoever without written permission from the author except in the case of brief quotations. For information, contact Sufficient Word Ministries: publisher@sufficientwordpublishing.com

Unless otherwise indicated, all Scripture quotations are taken from the KING JAMES VERSION of the Bible, public domain.

Scripture quotations marked (NKJV) have been taken from the Holy Bible, NEW KING JAMES VERSION®, Copyright © 1982 by Thomas Nelson, Inc. Used by permission. All rights reserved.

Scripture quotations marked (ISV) are taken from the Holy Bible: International Standard Version®. Copyright © 1996-forever by The ISV Foundation. All Rights Reserved Internationally. Used by permission.

Scripture quotations marked (NASB) are taken from the 1995 update of the New American Standard Bible®, Copyright © The Lockman Foundation 1960, 1962, 1963, 1968, 1971, 1972, 1973, 1975, 1977, 1995. Used by permission.

Scripture quotations marked (NIV) are taken from the Holy Bible, NEW INTERNATIONAL VERSION®, NIV® Copyright 1973, 1978, 1984, 2011 by Biblica, Inc.® Used by permission. All rights reserved worldwide.

Minnesota-Wisconsin Baptist Convention Leadership Team:
Dr. Leo Endel, Executive Director
Dr. Clint Calvert, Church Leadership Catalyst

Production and Design: Sufficient Word Ministries;
Madison Lux, *upwork.com/fl/madisonlux*

To order, send shipping address, contact information, and number of copies requested to publisher@sufficientwordpublishing.com

Minnesota-Wisconsin Edition: September 2023
ISBN: 978-1-946245-31-1

TABLE OF CONTENTS

Introduction	What's the Point?	1
Chapter 1	The Gospel By Which We Are Saved	5
Chapter 2	Who He Is	25
Chapter 3	What He Did	49
Chapter 4	Why I Need It	73
Chapter 5	How To Get It	93
Chapter 6	Where To Find It	121
Conclusion	What the Gospel Isn't	127
Appendix	Index of Objections	129

INTRODUCTION
WHAT'S THE POINT?

We, the authors, were both religious before we were Christian. As church-goers from church-going families, church attendance was expected, and we didn't think much more about it than that. If someone had asked either of us the purpose of going to church, we might have replied that God probably liked it when people learned about Him and sang about Him. We thought we were doing the right thing and pleasing Him. Most religion is like that; it is an attempt to please, appease, or gain favor with its god.

Eventually we became convinced that God was not particularly impressed that we showed up in a church building or sporadically tried to read and learn the Bible. We didn't understand much of what we read or heard about it, but from what we did understand of the Bible's message, we recognized that we didn't measure up. All those verses about loving and serving each other, about joyfulness regardless of circumstances and continual thankfulness—we knew that maintaining such things for any length of time was impossible. In short, we recognized that sinfulness was part of our nature.

Our religious tendencies led both of us to investigate other religions. The more we looked into Christianity, the more poorly the other religions fared in comparison. Some were oppressive, some seemed pointless, and some were even ridiculous. But Jesus seemed credible: His message was unique, and His story was both tragic and inspiring. He was not famous. He was poor. He preached in a small area for a few years, and then He died young. He should have vanished into obscurity, but instead, His contemporaries said His teachings "turned the world upside down." He claimed to fulfill the prophecies of ancient Jewish writings, and to be the only way to God. "Do more and try harder," was the message of religion, but Jesus said our religious efforts were vain. The uniqueness of that message was both perplexing and intriguing. Neither of us could turn away until we were convinced one way or the other.

We both began our faith journeys with respect for the Bible and a belief in an afterlife; the idea that after death it was just "lights out," was not even a consideration. Because of this conviction, we could see the reasonableness of a creator having some standards for entrance into His realm. We knew that we couldn't fix the wrongs that we had done in the past, and even if we improved, we still wouldn't have the perfection which the Bible says is required in heaven. It did seem reasonable that God would have to be the one to make us fit for His kingdom.

Arriving at the point of belief in Jesus' claims did take time. In our separate lives and in our own time—one of us had a two-year path, and one of us had a ten-year path—we made the connection between our continual shortcomings and Jesus' answers. Both of us heard the Gospel message, that Jesus Christ paid the price for the sins of mankind to save us from sin's punishment. According to this "good news," those who believed would spend eternity with God, rather than remain separated from Him because of sin. We each had our own questions, however, which had to be answered in order for us to come to faith.

Today, we remain convinced that there is a creator who provided an eternal destiny for those He created. We further believe that the Creator is the God of the Bible, and that He draws mankind into a relationship with Himself through the Gospel and through the convincing work of the Holy Spirit, as coming to faith is not merely an intellectual exercise. We believe that individuals have a choice to accept or to reject the Gospel message, and that God does not force anyone into a relationship with Him. We also believe that God has made efforts to make Himself known and knowable. Not everyone comes to the same conclusions, and we understand that. But we hope it is worth the time and effort to explore and consider the Christian message of "good news" also called "the Gospel of Christ." Perhaps you will come to believe it. We hope that this book will help you toward that end.

–Preston and Kelly

> *1 Moreover, brethren, I declare unto you the gospel which I preached unto you, which also ye have received, and wherein ye stand; 2 **By which also ye are saved**, if ye keep in memory what I preached unto you, unless ye have believed in vain. 3 For I delivered unto you first of all that which I also received, **how that Christ died for our sins according to the scriptures; 4 And that he was buried, and that he rose again the third day according to the scriptures**...* (1 Cor 15:1-4)

CHAPTER ONE
THE GOSPEL BY WHICH WE ARE SAVED

The Gospel of Christ

Moreover, brethren, I declare unto you the gospel which I preached unto you, which also ye have received, and wherein ye stand; 2 **By which also ye are saved,** *if ye keep in memory what I preached unto you, unless ye have believed in vain. 3 For I delivered unto you first of all that which I also received, how that Christ died for our sins according to the scriptures; 4 And that he was buried, and that he rose again the third day according to the scriptures: 5 And that he was seen of Cephas, then of the twelve: 6 After that, he was seen of above five hundred brethren at once; of whom the greater part remain unto this present, but some are fallen asleep. 7 After that, he was seen of James; then of all the apostles. 8 And last of all he was seen of me also, as of one born out of due time.* (1 Cor 15:1-8)

The Gospel message, or "good news" of Christianity, is contained in 1 Corinthians 15:1-8, which declares it to be the message by which one is saved. In Romans 1:16, this message is given a title by the Apostle Paul, who calls it "the Gospel of Christ," adding that it is "the power of God unto salvation." Although other verses such as John 3:16 and Ephesians 2:8-9 contain additional information about biblical salvation, 1 Corinthians 15:3-4 is the essential core of the Gospel, namely, the death, burial, and resurrection of Jesus Christ for our sins, and, therefore, contains the object of faith for the Christian.

For the purposes of this book, we most often refer to the Gospel as 1 Corinthians 15:1-4, because we believe that verses 1-2 are worthy of inclusion in an explanation of the Gospel. These verses identify the passage as the saving Gospel message and also provide a warning about "believing in vain," a factual belief without the intended purpose of salvation. In other words, one can simply believe some or all of the Bible as a historical narrative without further significance. Verses 5-8 of 1 Corinthians 15 are also significant because they record that the resurrection was verified by hundreds of witnesses.

We have labeled the five elements of the Gospel of Christ as who, what, why, how, and where. Here they are briefly described according to historical Christianity:

- **Who:** Jesus Christ, God the Son, the one and only Savior of sinners, and the one and only way of salvation.
- **What:** The death, burial, and resurrection of Jesus Christ on the cross for sins. Jesus died for the sins of mankind, taking upon Himself God's punishment for humanity's sins.
- **Why:** Jesus died as a substitute for humanity because every human being is a sinner and under penalty of death

for sinning against God. Finite human beings cannot "make up for" or "undo" their sins and are, therefore, facing eternal suffering in the lake of fire, the permanent residence of those who will pay for their own sins.
- **How:** One is saved from the penalty of sin by God's grace through faith in the Gospel. God graciously grants deliverance from sin's penalty to each who believes the Gospel of Christ, 1 Corinthians 15:1-4, and who does so for the purpose of his own salvation, apart from works of any kind.
- **Where:** Twice in the Gospel is the phrase, "according to the scriptures," a reference to the source of the saving message. Because the Bible is the revelation of Jesus Christ and the source of the Gospel, disbelief in the Bible can be a barrier to accepting the truth of its message.

In addition to the essential elements of the Gospel of Christ, there are several biblical teachings which help explain the Gospel. These include the meaning of spiritual birth, the substitutionary sacrifice of Jesus, man's position in the family of Adam, the placement of the believer into the body of Christ, the necessity of the faith system for salvation, and the Bible as God's written revelation of Himself.

The Source of the Gospel is the Bible

Creation itself reveals the existence of a Creator, but the general revelation of God's existence does not reveal His identity, nor how to enter into a relationship with Him. Although creation evidences a creator, more information is needed to know who God is. So, how can one know Him and know that His message is true? He provided two proofs of Himself: He dwelt with mankind in the person of Jesus Christ, and He provided a written record revealing Himself. Christians consider the Bible to be a trustworthy historical record which reveals God the Son and the message of salvation, the Gospel.

The Gospel of Christ, found in 1 Corinthians 15:1-4, contains the phrase "according to the scriptures" twice, suggesting that the trustworthiness of the source of the message is inextricable from the facts of the saving message. For this reason, we encourage you to consider your opinion of the Bible. You might hold a general respect for it as a significant historical and religious book. If you think otherwise, we hope you will evaluate the reason for your doubt. It is possible that you hold assumptions about the Bible's reliability, but have no evidence for doubting its testimony. Because Christians are convinced that the Bible is the very word of God, perhaps you would be open to learning why so many believe it. If you are, many books have been written for those who wish to know more about the supernatural origin of the Bible.

Christian Salvation is a Spiritual Birth

Throughout our years of ministry, we have found that the biblical concept of a spiritual birth is one that is not well understood, even among Christians. It is a unique teaching, one that was difficult for even a learned religious leader of Israel to understand:

> *Nicodemus saith unto him, How can a man be born when he is old? can he enter the second time into his mother's womb, and be born?* (Jn 3:4)

The importance of understanding the spiritual birth is for the purpose of distinguishing religious works or "good works" from spiritual salvation. Christianity stands alone in teaching that no one has ever been saved by law-keeping, living a clean life, or doing works of any kind. The Bible tells us instead that we *must* be "born again" (Jn 3:7). But Christians and non-Christians alike may hold views which make Christianity seem like a social activity or membership in a civic group. It is important to know that the Christian faith is not simply a lifestyle of goodness, giving, and church attendance. While morality, helpfulness, and other virtuous traits are meant to be products of a spiritual birth, there are many decent, philanthropic, community-minded non-Christians. Therefore, such outward traits do not define Christianity.

Helpful for comprehending the Christian spiritual birth is knowing more about birth and death according to the Bible. For example, the death of a person does not result in his annihilation or non-existence. When a person's physical body stops functioning, that person lives on. From the Christian perspective, death can, therefore, be viewed as a separation. The material part of man, the body, is in the grave, separated from the immaterial soul and spirit, which continue to live.

The human spirit is the part of man which can be connected to God. God is the only source of spiritual life, which is why we refer to our relationship with Him as spiritual. A person can be physically alive and yet be spiritually dead because he is separated from the source of spiritual life (Eph 2:1). To be spiritually born means that one's human spirit is in communion with, meaning connected with, God. Terms you may have heard or seen in the Bible which refer to the born-again spiritual condition include "the new birth," being "born from above," "begotten again," "indwelt," and "regenerated."

Paradise Lost

A brief history of human spiritual life begins with the first man, Adam, who was created sinless and in spiritual communion with God. God told Adam that if he ate from the tree of the knowledge of good and evil, he would die (Gen 3:3). But Adam did not drop dead upon eating its fruit. Although he *began* dying physically, his immediate death was spiritual. God could no longer commune with Adam's spirit because it was now tainted with sin.

When Adam ate from the tree, he was making a decision to act independently of God's will. His act of disobedience was sin, and, therefore, he became separated from a holy God who cannot commune with sin. Neither could God commune with any of Adam's descendants. Although Adam was created in the likeness of God, the Bible tells us that after he sinned, Adam's children were created in *his* likeness; they were sinners (Gen 5:1-3). Having sinned, Adam no longer possessed the quality of being spiritually alive and, therefore, could not pass on to his descendants that which he no longer had. As a result of being part of Adam's family, every human being is born separated from God, just as Adam became separated when he rebelled in the garden (Gen 3:6). This is why every person is born a sinner, and why the Bible refers to the human race as being "in Adam," a doctrine we will cover later in this chapter.

The intimate spiritual connection enjoyed by Adam could not be restored until sin no longer stood between God and man. The restoration of spiritual communion was accomplished when God the Son died for sin on the cross (Ro 5:10; 2 Cor 5:18-19). With all sin having been paid, God can now commune with any man who has accepted Jesus' payment for his own sins (1 Cor 15:22).

In summary, Christianity teaches that all men are born spiritually dead, separated from God by sin, and in need of a savior. To escape the punishment for sin, each must be cleansed from sin by accepting the payment made on his behalf by Jesus. Upon believing the Gospel, one is no longer separated from God by sin, but saved from damnation, made part of a spiritual family, able to enjoy a relationship with God, and destined for heaven. Christians are called to share the message of the Gospel of Christ, so that each who hears may decide for himself if he believes it.

Jesus Christ is God the Son, the One and Only Savior of Mankind

Understanding the spiritual nature of the Christian faith is necessary in order to distinguish being "born again" from the religious activities or good works required by other religions. The identity of the man whom Christians consider their Savior is another important component of the Gospel message. Although the Gospel verses do not plainly say "Jesus is God," the testimony of other Bible verses is the reason that Christians believe that Jesus is God the Son. From the Christian perspective, if Jesus were simply a man and not God, placing one's faith in an ordinary man cannot save anyone, even if that man was an extraordinary example of altruism, forgiveness, and love.

Some people who hear the Gospel do not know the significance of Jesus being more than a man. An ordinary man, however, has no way to pay for the sins of others; he would have his own to pay for. His death on a cross would not solve the problem of sin between God and man because it would be followed by the penalty God requires for every man: eternal separation in the lake of fire (Rev 20:15). For Jesus to be God the Savior, and able to accomplish what the Gospel claims, He would have to be unique. He could not have been some great guy who died to set an example of sacrificial love or to make a statement about forgiveness, as some believe.

If you agree with the Bible's assessment that humanity has a sin problem, its size and seriousness is a matter of infinite proportions. Because an infinite God has been offended by an infinite number of sins, either the offender will spend infinity paying for sin (Rev 20:10-14), or the payment for sin must be made by an infinite person. This is the reason that the Savior must be God.

But the Savior must also be a man. To justly stand as a substitute for mankind, only a man could die for sins. Only a man could be the replacement for Adam as the head of the human family. According to the Bible, Jesus is the only one who fulfills both requirements: He is fully God, who took on a human nature and body to become fully man also (Phil 2:6, Col 2:9, Heb 2:6). In so doing, He was both a just and an infinite substitutionary sacrifice for the sins of mankind in making Himself the recipient of God's punishment.

Not only does the Bible present Jesus as God in the flesh, He is declared to be the one and only Savior of mankind. The Christian Gospel is not compatible with, "You have your way; I have mine." Because of Jesus' exclusive claims, one cannot believe that there are other "saviors" or other ways to be saved while at the same time believing the Gospel message (Acts 4:12, Jn 8:12, 10:9, 14:6). A person who considers Jesus to be one religious prophet, messenger, or savior among other equally valid ways to God does not believe in the Jesus Christ of the Bible. Faith in a false "Jesus" is vain, meaning it is of no use for the purpose of saving. The object of saving faith, according to Christianity, must be the correct object, namely, Jesus Christ, God the Son, the Savior of the world (1 Cor 15:2, 2 Cor 11:4).

Jesus Paid for Sins by Dying on a Cross

Jesus is at the center of the Gospel message. Christianity teaches that to be saved, one must believe in what Jesus did: that He died for sins on a cross, was buried, and on the third day He rose again, according to the scriptures. You may wonder what that act accomplished and why it needed to be done. For example, many people died on crosses; what was different about this death? Why was a cross the method of Jesus' death and what did it achieve?

Jesus had to die because the shedding of blood is the method that God chose for paying a debt to Him. Leviticus 17:11 informs us that life is in the blood, and we know that losing one's blood is certain death. Hebrews 9:22 teaches that without the shedding of blood is no remission, referring to the remission of sins. We see blood sacrifice after mankind's fall into sin in Genesis 4:3-5 and in the Law of Moses, detailed in Leviticus. When God the Son came to earth to be a sacrifice for all mankind, He took on a human body and shed His blood, giving His life for ours.

Jesus' death was unique because it fulfilled prophecy, allowing Jesus to be identified by the nation of Israel as its Messiah. The Bible does not explain why God chose crucifixion as the manner of death, but this horrific method does seem to highlight the seriousness of sin. Under the law, dying on a tree signified being cursed by God, pointing to what the Bible says is the destiny of sinners (Deut 21:22-23, Gal 3:13, Jn 3:18).

Looking again to the first man, Adam, we can discover what Jesus' death achieved. The Bible teaches that Adam was the first man, and was the head of the human race. It describes mankind as born "in Adam," meaning we are under his headship and part of his family. Because Adam sinned, all his descendants are reckoned by

God to be sinners "in Adam," and are therefore disqualified from communing with God.

In 1 Corinthians 15:45, Jesus is called the "last Adam." 1 Corinthians 15:22 states, "For as in Adam all die, even so in Christ shall all be made alive." Jesus became Adam's substitute as head of the human race; when God the Father poured out His wrath against sin onto Jesus Christ, making Him sin for us, He was moving the accountability for humanity's sin to its new head, Jesus (2 Cor 5:21). The Apostle Paul explains in his letter to the church in Rome that Jesus' payment for sins reconciles sinners to God (Ro 5:8-10). Because Jesus' sacrifice for sin paid the debt originally incurred by Adam and took the punishment which we all deserve for our sins, sin no longer stands between God and man. A spiritual connection with God has once again been made possible.

Not only is the believer in Christ spiritually born and reconciled to God; he is credited with Christ's righteousness and transferred from the human family of Adam to the spiritual family of God. These spiritual transactions happen in the mind of God; it is not something we can see. This new spiritual location is known as the Christian's position "in Christ," and the placing of a person there is known as Holy Spirit baptism. The new spiritual entity created is called "the body of Christ" and has Christ as its head instead of Adam (Ro 6:3; 1 Cor12:13).

According to the Christian Gospel, Jesus suffered on the cross the punishment that man deserved for offending God. Jesus' death achieved our salvation because He paid both the physical and the spiritual price for sin, just as Adam did. Jesus was a physical human substitute for mankind, replacing the first man, Adam, as the representative of the human race, and physically dying in our place for sin. Having been "made sin for us" and declared guilty of the sins of the world, He was also the object of God's wrath in the spiritual punishment for our sins, spiritually forsaken, separated from fellowship with God the Father and the Holy Spirit while He hung on the cross. Understanding the purpose and significance of Jesus' substitutionary sacrifice might answer questions which would otherwise be a barrier to trusting in it for salvation.

For he hath made him to be sin for us, who knew no sin; that we might be made the righteousness of God in him. (2 Cor 5:21)

… My God, my God, why hast thou forsaken me? (Mt 27:46b, see also Mk 15:34)

Salvation from Sin is Accessed by Faith

The Bible teaches that every person is a sinner who is in need of a savior from sin. It says that Jesus Christ, God the Son, is that Savior, and His offer of reconciliation with God is accessed through belief in the Gospel of Christ, found in 1 Corinthians 15:1-4.

Believing the Gospel is also known as having faith in it. To have faith means to be persuaded that something is true and, therefore, to trust in it (Ro 4:21; Heb 11:13). Regarding faith for salvation, the Apostle Paul tells us, "It is by faith that it might be by grace" (Ro 4:16). The word "grace" can be translated as "undeserved favor," and receiving a favor is the opposite of working to earn something. Because we cannot both receive a gift and work to earn it, grace is contrasted with work. As an illustration, when I work, my employer is indebted to me, meaning I am owed wages for that work (Ro 4:4). The wages I earn are not a gift. However, when something is a gift of grace, it was not earned and not even deserved; it was just given. The Bible teaches that salvation is a freely given gift from God to any who will believe and freely receive it. Referring to Adam's sin and Christ's worthy sacrifice on the cross to provide eternal life, the Apostle Paul writes:

> *Therefore as by the offence of one, judgment came upon all men to condemnation; even so by the righteousness of one, the free gift came upon all men unto justification of life.* (Ro 5:18)

It is important to note that there is no merit that I can claim for myself in recognizing what someone else has accomplished. Therefore, when I believe in what Christ did, I am not indebting God to me as I would if I had earned what I received. My faith in the death, burial, and resurrection of Jesus Christ upon the cross for sin is a *belief*, and has nothing whatsoever to do with my acumen, abilities, or achievements. In faith, I am looking away from myself to the work of another; I am trusting Him, and in what He did for me. Therefore, what I receive in return for my faith is gracious: I owe nothing for it. Because God loved me in Christ, in that spiritual transaction on the cross, He can freely give me the gift of salvation when I place my faith in the Gospel message (Ro 5:15-18, 6:23; Eph 2:8-9, Titus 3:5a). In believing the Gospel, I am accepting what He did out of His love, and mercy, and goodness.

Any belief in works must be eliminated in order to accept the Gospel of Christ by faith. Just as it did in the garden, even one sin would separate me from God and disqualify me from earning salvation by good works. It is only by the faith system that God can provide salvation, so that it can be given as a free gift, by grace. It must be so, as no man could ever earn it.

Acts 13: The Apostle Paul Explains the Gospel

The Gospel message contains a savior who died on a cross for sins, was buried, and rose from the dead in accordance with biblical prophecies. Although the Gospel contains these necessary elements, it is not simply a formula to which we give a nod. Often, the Gospel needs some explanation. The most thorough record of Paul presenting the Gospel is found in Acts 13:15-44, where he is speaking to a group of Jews. This passage includes some background information from the Old Testament which is specific to the Jewish audience, followed by the basics of the Gospel and many of its supporting truths. We have included brief comments and added emphasis in some verses.

15 And after the reading of the law and the prophets the rulers of the synagogue sent unto them, saying, Ye men and brethren, if ye have any word of exhortation for the people, say on. 16 Then Paul stood up, and beckoning with his hand said, Men of Israel, and ye that fear God, give audience. 17 The God of this people of Israel chose our fathers, and exalted the people when they dwelt as strangers in the land of Egypt, and with an high arm brought he them out of it. 18 And about the time of forty years suffered he their manners in the wilderness. 19 And when he had destroyed seven nations in the land of Canaan, he divided their land to them by lot. 20 And after that he gave unto them judges about the space of four hundred and fifty years, until Samuel the prophet. 21 And afterward they desired a king: and God gave unto them Saul the son of Cis, a man of the tribe of Benjamin, by the space of forty years. 22 And when he had removed him, he raised up unto them David to be their king; to whom also he gave testimony, and said, I have found David the son of Jesse, a man after mine own heart, which shall fulfil all my will.

23 Of this man's seed hath God according to his promise raised unto Israel a Saviour, Jesus: 24 When John had first preached before his coming the baptism of repentance to all the people of Israel.

Jesus, the Savior, from the seed of David, as prophesied to Israel.

*25 And as John fulfilled his course, he said, Whom think ye that I am? I am not he. But, behold, there cometh one after me, whose shoes of his feet I am not worthy to loose. 26 Men and brethren, children of the stock of Abraham, and **whosoever** among you feareth God, to you is the word of this salvation sent.*

This message is the saving message, available to all.

27 For they that dwell at Jerusalem, and their rulers, because they knew him not, nor yet the voices of the prophets which are read every sabbath day, they have fulfilled them in condemning him.

28 And though they found no cause of death in him, yet desired they Pilate that he should be slain.	Jesus was an innocent substitute.
29 And when they had fulfilled all that was written of him, they took him down from the tree, and laid him in a sepulchre.	Jesus fulfilled all the prophecies about Him, according to the scriptures.
*30 But God raised him from the dead: 31 And he was seen many days of them which came up with him from Galilee to Jerusalem, who are his witnesses unto the people. 32 And we declare unto you **glad tidings,** how that the promise which was made unto the fathers, 33 God hath fulfilled the same unto us their children, in that he hath raised up Jesus again;*	This is the "good news," or gospel, that Jesus died on a tree, was buried and physically resurrected, all witnessed.
	God kept His promises to the Jewish nation.
as it is also written in the second psalm, Thou art my Son, this day have I begotten thee.	Jesus is God the Son, deity.
34 And as concerning that he raised him up from the dead, now no more to return to corruption, he said on this wise, I will give you the sure mercies of David.	

*35 Wherefore he saith also in another psalm, Thou shalt not suffer thine **Holy One** to see corruption. 36 For David, after he had served his own generation by the will of God, fell on sleep, and was laid unto his fathers, and saw corruption: 37 But he, whom God raised again, saw no corruption.*

God's Old Testament title is used, connecting this "good news" with the Jewish prophecies. Jesus was sinless and could not be held by death.

*38 Be it known unto you therefore, men and brethren, that through **this man** is preached unto you the forgiveness of sins: 39 And by him all that believe are justified from all things, from which ye could not be justified by the law of Moses.*

Jesus is a real man. Forgiveness from sin is accessed by faith, not by law. Jesus' payment is sufficient for all sins, providing security to those who believe.

40 Beware therefore, lest that come upon you, which is spoken of in the prophets; 41 Behold, ye despisers, and wonder, and perish: for I work a work in your days, a work which ye shall in no wise believe, though a man declare it unto you. 42 And when the Jews were gone out of the synagogue, the Gentiles besought that these words might be preached to them the next sabbath.

*43 Now when the congregation was broken up, many of the Jews and religious proselytes followed Paul and Barnabas: who, speaking to them, **persuaded** them to continue in the grace of God. 44 And the next sabbath day came almost the whole city together to hear the word of God.* Acts 13:15-44

The will of man is moved by urging: persuasion was used to reason with the hearers about the truth of this message.

What Paul's presentation does not contain is as important as what it does contain. For example, there is no call to do anything. False versions of Christianity add requirements of good works or religious acts to the Gospel, and doing so negates grace. As previously noted, works and grace are opposites. Considering, for example, the popularity of Christian baptismal ceremonies and the variety of meanings attached to them, it is noteworthy that in Acts 13 only John's baptism of repentance for Israel is mentioned; water baptism for Christians is not mentioned, required, or practiced, nor is any other addition or human effort. The Gospel of Christ is simply a message to be believed.

Respecting Human Will

Christians share the Gospel of Christ, found in 1 Corinthians 15:1-4, out of obedience to God and concern for the eternal destiny of souls. While we believe that refusing the Gospel is a tragedy of eternal consequence, it is God who allows His creatures to reject Him, and it is not part of our calling to give the impression that we are trying to take that choice away. God protects each person's right to exercise freedom.

Christians you know may have presented you with the Gospel prior to now. You may have listened, but needed time to give thought and consideration to what you heard. Perhaps hearing the Gospel led to questions that have not been answered, or perhaps you were not yet ready to consider Christianity. Sometimes more of life needs to happen; just getting older, and losing things, and losing people tends to cause a person to think differently about eternity. Many of us do not care to think about death and what lies beyond until we must face it ourselves or deal with the loss of another.

You may not believe parts of the Bible or any of it, but the Bible claims to be the word of God. Each person may decide whether or not he believes it. Our goal in this book is to simply and plainly testify to what the Bible says regarding salvation and to answer questions about it. If you are willing to think about what you already know and believe about salvation, then you can compare it with what scripture teaches about who God is, what He did, why He did it, and how to get it. Doing so can help you clarify your convictions in regard to the Gospel message.

As both of us once did, you may have at one time in your life made a profession of faith in the Gospel of Christ, but feel no peace or assurance of your salvation. Perhaps you had a good intention to do God's will, so you responded to an altar call or prayed a suggested prayer. It is possible that when you did this, you did not understand the Gospel. If this is the case, we want to help you to be certain that you are a Christian because the Gospel is true and you believe it, and not for any other reason. Even if you have not considered the Gospel message at all, we, the authors, hope to give you a reason to do so now. According to the Bible, salvation is available by simple faith in the death, burial, and resurrection of Jesus Christ for the purpose of salvation from sins. Arriving there, however, can be surprisingly difficult because of the numerous ways that the salvation message has been misconstrued. Therefore, in the following chapters we provide Bible verses and brief explanations to answer the many possible objections that a person might have in regard to the Gospel. It is our intention to enable any person who wishes to know or to better understand the Gospel message to be able to do so.

CHAPTER TWO

WHO HE IS

God and the Person of Jesus Christ

For in him dwelleth all the fulness of the Godhead bodily. (Col 2:9)

The Gospel of Christ, found in 1 Corinthians 15:1-4, contains five elements which we refer to as who, what, why, how, and where. All five tell us something about Christianity's savior, Jesus Christ. Jesus is the one who died on a cross. He died as a sacrifice for sin because, according to the Bible, every person is born in need of salvation from sin. Salvation is accessed by faith in Jesus' work on the cross for sins, and the source of these truths is the Bible, the revelation of Jesus Christ, God the Son to mankind. These five elements are essential to Christian salvation.

Because Jesus' sacrifice on the cross is the object of biblical saving faith, who Jesus is must necessarily be central to the Gospel message. Objections to "who He is" may be in regard to Jesus in particular or to God in general, such as to God's triune nature, His attributes, or His character. Some take issue with Jesus' deity, considering Him a sort of "God-Junior" or merely a created being. Others do not recognize the differences between the God of the Bible and the deities of false religion, the movies, or their own imaginations.

Those who believe the record of the Bible believe the testimony of Israel's prophets who proclaimed that God was their Savior. The New Testament revealed to the world that God the Savior was the man known as Jesus of Nazareth. God had taken on a human body and human nature, while never ceasing to be God. This is known as the incarnation.

According to Christian belief, placing one's faith in a false God or a false Jesus does not save. Therefore, in order to consider Christianity's claims regarding deliverance from sin and eternal life, you need to know who Jesus is, and who the God of the Bible is also. Because of the many mischaracterizations and misunderstandings about the God of the Bible, and about Jesus in particular, we hope that this chapter will help clarify and explain questions you may have about who He is.

1

"Jesus isn't God! He was just..." (...a teacher, a prophet, a good man.)

And Thomas answered and said unto Him, My Lord and my God. (Jn 20:28)

The Bible presents Jesus as divine, the unique Son of God. Christians believe that Jesus Christ is fully and eternally God. He is one of three divine persons who comprise what is known as the Godhead. A common objection to this teaching is that Jesus is a lesser being than God, some kind of being created by God, or simply a man who was a moral teacher or a prophet. The New Testament presents Jesus as the prophesied Savior, and the Old Testament teaches that Israel's Savior is God:

> Yet I am the LORD thy God from the land of Egypt, and thou shalt know no god but me: for there is no saviour beside me. (Hos 13:4)

Additionally, the Gospel of the Apostle John teaches that "the Word" is a title for Jesus Christ, who is both God and the Creator.

> In the beginning was the Word, and the Word was with God, and the Word was God. The same was in the beginning with God. All things were made by him; and without him was not any thing made that was made. (Jn 1:1-3)

Jesus' own statement that He is one with the Father was a claim to be God. This claim, although perhaps not obvious to modern readers, was perfectly clear to the Jews, who were enraged by it:

> I and my Father are one. Then the Jews took up stones again to stone him. Jesus answered them, Many good works have I shewed you from my Father; for which of those works do ye stone me? The Jews answered him, saying, For a good work we stone thee not; but for blasphemy; and because that thou, being a man, makest thyself God. (Jn 10:30-33)

Jesus did things that God would do. He performed miracles such as commanding the elements; He accepted worship, and He forgave sins:

> And he saith unto them, Why are ye fearful, O ye of little faith? Then he arose, and rebuked the winds and the sea; and

there was a great calm. But the men marvelled, saying, What manner of man is this, that even the winds and the sea obey him! (Mt 8:26-27)

And as they went to tell his disciples, behold, Jesus met them, saying, All hail. And they came and held him by the feet, and worshipped him. (Mt 28:9)

Whether is it easier to say to the sick of the palsy, Thy sins be forgiven thee; or to say, Arise, and take up thy bed, and walk? (Mk 2:9)

In addition to His words and deeds, Jesus' birth, ministry, and death fulfilled hundreds of biblical prophecies. Among them is one which calls His name Immanuel, meaning, "God with us."

Therefore the Lord himself shall give you a sign; Behold, a virgin shall conceive, and bear a son, and shall call his name Immanuel. (Isa 7:14)

Colossians contains one of the most descriptive passages about the deity of Jesus Christ, describing Him as the Savior from sin, the very likeness of God, and the eternal Creator. Speaking of God the Father, and Jesus, who is God the Son, the Apostle Paul writes:

Who hath delivered us from the power of darkness, and hath translated us into the kingdom of his dear Son: In whom we have redemption through his blood, even the forgiveness of sins: Who is the image of the invisible God, the firstborn of every creature: For by him were all things created, that are in heaven, and that are in earth, visible and invisible, whether they be thrones, or dominions, or principalities, or powers: all things were created by him, and for him: And he is before all things, and by him all things consist. And he is the head of the body, the church: who is the beginning, the firstborn from the dead; that in all things he might have the preeminence. (Col 1:13-18)

Jesus declared Himself "I am," a reference to His self-existent nature. This is the name that God revealed to Moses:

And God said unto Moses, I AM THAT I AM: and he said, Thus shalt thou say unto the children of Israel, I AM hath sent me unto you. (Ex 3:14)

That is why I told you that you will die in your sins, for unless you believe that I AM, you'll die in your sins. (Jn 8:24 ISV)

I'm telling you this now, before it happens, so that when it does happen, you may believe that I AM. (Jn 13:19 ISV)

Jesus said unto them, Verily, verily, I say unto you, Before Abraham was, I am. (Jn 8:58)

It is important that Jesus is a man; He had to take on a human nature and body and become fully man for two reasons. Firstly, only a man could be a substitute for Adam as head of the human race. Secondly, only a man could be a just substitute to receive the penalty for men's sins. But according to the Bible, Jesus is not merely a man. The testimony of scripture is that Jesus is God the Son, the Creator, the I AM, and the fulfillment of the Old Testament prophecies that a savior would come. For these reasons, Christians believe that Jesus Christ is fully God and fully man.

_____

_____

_____

2

"God is not a trinity. The word isn't even in the Bible."

> ...*in the name of the Father, and the Son, and the Holy Spirit*... (Mt 28:19b NASB)

Some find the concept of God as a trinity to be problematic; it is difficult to understand, unique to Christianity, and not a word found in scripture. Although the word "trinity" is not in the Bible, it is a word Christians use in order to describe a biblical concept. Some who deny the Trinity claim that God is a singular entity who has three "roles" or "forms." Such an explanation does not hold up when members of the Godhead refer to one another. Jesus said:

> *A little while, and ye shall not see me: and again, a little while, and ye shall see me, because I go to the Father.* (Jn 16:16)

> *But the Comforter, which is the Holy Ghost, whom the Father will send in my name, he shall teach you all things, and bring all things to your remembrance, whatsoever I have said unto you.* (Jn 14:26)

> *But when the Comforter is come, whom I will send unto you from the Father, even the Spirit of truth, which proceedeth from the Father, he shall testify of me...* (Jn 15:26)

The Father spoke and said:

> *And lo a voice from heaven, saying, This is my beloved Son, in whom I am well pleased.* (Mt 3:17)

Also supporting the doctrine of the Trinity are passages which make reference to all three persons in the Godhead:

Elect according to the foreknowledge of God the Father, through sanctification of the Spirit, unto obedience and sprinkling of the blood of Jesus Christ: Grace unto you, and peace, be multiplied. (1 Pet 1:2)

And be not drunk with wine, wherein is excess; but be filled with the Spirit; Speaking to yourselves in psalms and hymns and spiritual songs, singing and making melody in your heart to the Lord; Giving thanks always for all things unto God and the Father in the name of our Lord Jesus Christ. (Eph 5:18-20)

For through him (Jesus Christ) *we both have access by one Spirit unto the Father.* (Eph 2:18, clarification added)

Come ye near unto me, hear ye this; I have not spoken in secret from the beginning; from the time that it was, there am I: and now the Lord GOD, and his Spirit, hath sent me. Thus saith the LORD, thy Redeemer, the Holy One of Israel; I am the LORD thy God which teacheth thee to profit, which leadeth thee by the way that thou shouldest go. (Isa 48:16-17)

For unto us a child is born, unto us a son is given: and the government shall be upon his shoulder: and his name shall be called Wonderful, Counsellor, The mighty God, The everlasting Father, The Prince of Peace. (Isa 9:6)

A subtle revelation of the Trinity can be found in the biblical use of pronouns, such as in Genesis chapter 1. When Moses refers to God, he uses the singular words "his" and "he." When describing the persons of God communicating amongst themselves, the plural "us" is used:

> *And God said, Let **us** make man in **our** image, after **our** likeness: and let them have dominion over the fish of the sea, and over the fowl of the air, and over the cattle, and over all the earth, and over every creeping thing that creepeth upon the earth. So God created man in **his** own image, in the image of God created **he** him; male and female created **he** them."*
> (Gen 1:26-27)

It is difficult to describe the Trinity because there is nothing and no one else like God, but it can help to compare Him to something we understand, such as humankind. We will refer to the kind of being that God is as "God-kind."

There is only one being that can be classified as God-kind; there is no other like Him. If we compare the substance of God-kind with that of humankind, we know that each member of humankind exists in an individual human body which is made of matter. God-kind, however, is spirit. Spirit is what He is made of; it is the substance of His being.

God reveals Himself as being one and also as existing in three persons. When God is described as being one, it means that He is one spirit, the only one of His kind. God-kind is also a trinity, referring to the fact that three persons share one spirit. The persons of God are not separate individuals existing independently from one another as humans do. God is unique: one God in three persons.

The unity of God, meaning that God is one spirit, is taught in scripture:

> *And Jesus answered him, The first of all the commandments is, Hear, O Israel; The Lord our God is one Lord...* (Mk 12:29)

> *Thou believest that there is one God; thou doest well: the devils also believe, and tremble.* (Jas 2:19)
>
> *God is Spirit: and those who worship him must worship in spirit and truth.* (Jn 4:24 NSAB)

Additional support for the Trinity is that all three divine persons are called "God." The Father is God:

> *Blessed be God, even the Father of our Lord Jesus Christ, the Father of mercies, and the God of all comfort.* (2 Cor 1:3)
>
> *And that every tongue should confess that Jesus Christ is Lord, to the glory of God the Father.* (Phil 2:11)

The second person of the Trinity, the Son, is God:

> *In the beginning was the Word, and the Word was with God, and the Word was God.* (Jn 1:1)
>
> *For in him* (Jesus Christ) *dwelleth all the fulness of the Godhead bodily.* (Col 2:9, clarification added)

The third person of the Trinity, the Holy Spirit, is God:

> *But Peter said, Ananias, why hath Satan filled thine heart to lie to the Holy Ghost, and to keep back part of the price of the land? Whiles it remained, was it not thine own? and after it was sold, was it not in thine own power? why hast thou conceived this thing in thine heart? thou hast not lied unto men, but unto God.* (Acts 5:3-4)
>
> *The Spirit of the Lord spake by me, and his word was in my tongue.* (2 Sam 23:2)

The Trinity is a complex doctrine of Christianity. Our intention in this book is to allow the Bible to speak for itself to describe God, and what He provided for salvation. If you are considering this or other Christian teachings, you do not have to take our word for it, but can read and study these and other verses in order to decide for yourself if you believe the biblical record.

3
"The Bible has two different gods: an angry, punitive god in the Old Testament, and a kind and forgiving Jesus in the New Testament. These cannot be the same God, so I don't believe."

For I am the LORD, I change not... (Mal 3:6a)

Another objection to "who He is" comes from the perception that Jesus in the New Testament of the Bible is different from the God described in the Old Testament. We do not deny that there are some differences, but it is not because there are different Gods being described. Seeming differences only reflect the various aspects of God's character, and different stages of His eternal program shown throughout scripture. That God is not one-dimensional is apparent when the whole counsel of scripture is considered. Looking only at a few passages may give an unbalanced portrayal. For example, Jesus is sometimes incorrectly characterized as a mild-mannered pacifist, but we see that He expressed righteous anger and had harsh words for many:

> *And they come to Jerusalem: and Jesus went into the temple, and began to cast out them that sold and bought in the temple, and overthrew the tables of the moneychangers, and the seats of them that sold doves; And would not suffer that any man should carry any vessel through the temple. And he taught, saying unto them, Is it not written. My house shall be called of all nations the house of prayer? But ye have made it a den of thieves!* (Mk 11:15-17)

> *But woe unto you, scribes and Pharisees, hypocrites! for ye shut up the kingdom of heaven against men: for ye neither go in yourselves, neither suffer ye them that are entering to go in.* (Matt 23:13)

> *The same day there came certain of the Pharisees, saying unto him, Get thee out, and depart hence: for Herod will kill thee. And he said unto them, Go ye, and tell that fox, Behold, I cast out devils, and I do cures to day and to morrow, and the third day I shall be perfected.* (Luke 13:31-32)

Likewise, Old Testament verses are sometimes used to portray God as angry and punitive. What we see, however, is that in His dealings with Adam and Eve, those of Noah's time, the people of Nineveh, rebellious Israel, and many others, God is patient and merciful. Psalm 145 contains one of many beautiful Old Testament tributes to God's character amid the repeated failings of His chosen nation Israel:

> *The LORD is gracious, and full of compassion; slow to anger, and of great mercy. The LORD is good to all: and his tender mercies are over all his works.* (Ps 145:8-9)

> *As the mountains are round about Jerusalem, so the LORD is round about his people from henceforth even for ever.* (Ps 125:2)

> *And rend your heart, and not your garments, and turn unto the LORD your God: for he is gracious and merciful, slow to anger, and of great kindness, and repenteth him of the evil.* (Joel 2:13)

God's character is perfectly balanced; He is kind and loving as well as just. In His perfect justice, He sometimes dispenses discipline and punishment, but that does not make Him a different God than Jesus, who is God the Son. Because God is teaching mankind different lessons at various times in history, some Bible portions put a greater emphasis on a particular aspect of God's character. An example of one of God's lessons to humanity is that He is holy and we are sinful. Referring to the Law of Moses, the Apostle Paul explains God's purpose in administrating Israel with a legal system:

> *Therefore by the deeds of the law there shall no flesh be justified in his sight: for by the law is the knowledge of sin.* (Ro 3:20)

Under God's perfect law system, the failings of man were made clear, thereby displaying the holiness of God in contrast. Providing evidence that humanity is sinful was meant to illuminate man's need for a savior. When the Savior came, the Apostle John tells us that Jesus' ministry had a different purpose than did the Law:

> *For the law was given by Moses, but grace and truth came by Jesus Christ.* (Jn 1:17)

Jesus' ministry was to display God's grace, culminating in His death on a cross to pay for the sins of the world. In the New Testament, we do not see a different god, or a change in God; what we see is a new chapter in God's plan and a new administration over His people. Recognizing the unfolding revelation within the Bible is crucial to understanding it.

_____

_____

_____

4

"God is love, and a loving God would not send anyone to hell."

And in hell he lift up his eyes, being in torments, and seeth Abraham afar off, and Lazarus in his bosom. (Lk 16:23)

In some cases, an objection to who God is, is due to a misunderstanding of His good character. Denying the consequence of sin is an example of this because it denies God's holiness. Objecting to hell by protesting that "God is love" misses the point that failing to judge sin is the equivalent of approving of it. Yes, God is love, but He is also just, always acting rightly. A human judge who let a convicted murderer go unpunished would not be considered to be performing an act of love, but one of corruption for failing to dispense justice. Because God's character is balanced between His loving kindness and His holy justice, He cannot ignore sin. Therefore, He has provided a solution to the problem of sin which is free, available to all, and recorded in the Gospel of Christ, 1 Corinthians 15:1-4.

God's holiness was emphasized under the Law of Moses, which clearly and continually revealed God's high expectations and the sinful failings of mankind:

> *And Joshua said unto the people, Ye cannot serve the LORD: for he is an holy God; he is a jealous God; he will not forgive your transgressions nor your sins. If ye forsake the LORD, and serve strange gods, then he will turn and do you hurt, and consume you, after that he hath done you good.* (Josh 24:19-20)

> *Sanctify yourselves therefore, and be ye holy: for I am the LORD your God. And ye shall keep my statutes, and do them: I am the LORD which sanctify you.* (Lev 20:7-8)

God asked His people to act in accordance with His holiness, but their disobedience revealed the need for a savior from sin. In the New Testament, the Savior was provided, and God's grace was displayed:

> *And the Word was made flesh, and dwelt among us, (and we beheld his glory, the glory as of the only begotten of the Father,) full of grace and truth.* (Jn 1:14)

> *For the law was given by Moses, but grace and truth came by Jesus Christ.* (Jn 1:17)

> *If we confess our sins, he is faithful and just to forgive us our sins, and to cleanse us from all unrighteousness.* (1 Jn 1:9)

The Gospel shows God's provision to satisfy both His holiness and His love for mankind. His holiness was satisfied by pouring out the punishment for sin upon a substitute for mankind, the person of Jesus Christ. God's love was satisfied by offering to all mankind a payment for sins, by faith in the death, burial, and resurrection of Jesus Christ. We surely cannot consider ourselves superior to God in our judgment and mercy. But that is the position taken when one denies the necessity of a consequence for sin. Denying the historical record of the Bible is to put oneself in the position of Bible expert, and to attack the honesty of Jesus, who spoke of hell many times. According to the Bible, Jesus is God in the flesh and our savior from hell. If that is so, He was not misinformed or lying when He warned His listeners of judgment to come:

> *And if thy right hand offend thee, cut it off, and cast it from thee: for it is profitable for thee that one of thy members should perish, and not that thy whole body should be cast into hell.* (Mt 5:30)
>
> *Ye serpents, ye generation of vipers, how can ye escape the damnation of hell?* (Mt 23:33)

The Bible teaches that because of who He is, God will ultimately provide justice for all, and because of His love and mercy, He has also provided a solution to the problem of sin. It also says that His desire is that none should perish but rather that all should come to repentance (2 Pet 3:9). God does not force anyone to spend eternity with Him, so each of us is allowed to consider the biblical call to believe the Gospel.

5

"There is too much suffering and evil in the world. I reject a God who allows it!"

These things I have spoken unto you, that in me ye might have peace. In the world ye shall have tribulation: but be of good cheer; I have overcome the world. (Jn 16:33)

The suffering seen in the world is a cause for sorrow. It might seem reasonable to blame God, who should be able to stop the evil and make everything better. The Bible promises hope for the future, so why does God not bring that future sooner? The reason is that if Christ had returned 100 years ago, millions of Christians alive today would never have been born. In what the Bible calls "the longsuffering of God," God is patiently waiting for every person who will come to believe the Gospel to do so, providing the opportunity for many more to be saved and to enjoy a perfect eternity. This is also why He does not instantly banish those who practice evil, because any one of them could believe and be saved. He does not necessarily stop the wicked behavior of men because He is the one who has given us choices about how to behave. Without choice, we cannot choose to love Him, which is His ultimate goal for each of us, according to the Bible. It says that God showed His love for us through Jesus' sacrifice of Himself "while we were yet sinners" (Ro 5:8). Lastly, in regard to evil, let us not forget that there are earthly consequences for our choices, which wicked people often reap.

Christians enjoy the comfort of a hope beyond this world: It is the promise of a perfect future for those who believe the Gospel. This world has many problems, but faith in the Gospel *is* the biblical solution, providing freedom from the power of sin. Objecting to the Gospel because of the suffering of mankind is a denial that God is good, and a displacement of the cause of suffering. God is the easy target of blame for this world's troubles, but He is not the one causing them. Suffering did not exist when God created the earth; what He created was good:

And God saw everything that he had made, and, behold, it was very good. (Gen 1:31a)

The God of the Bible says that He not only provides for His children; He even provides for those who reject Him:

That ye may be the children of your Father which is in heaven: for he maketh his sun to rise on the evil and on the good, and sendeth rain on the just and on the unjust. (Mt 5:45)

God helps His children when asked. He offers a moral code that, when followed, allows us to avoid many calamities. He fulfills prophecy which provides assurance that He always keeps His word.

And this is the confidence that we have in him, that, if we ask any thing according to his will, he heareth us... (1 Jn 5:14)

And we know that all things work together for good to them that love God, to them who are the called according to his purpose. (Ro 8:28)

For whatsoever things were written aforetime were written for our learning, that we through patience and comfort of the scriptures might have hope. (Ro 15:4)

Some of the world's problems are due to the curse of sin. God did curse the earth (Gen 3:17-19), but He also provided a solution to sin and a future free from its evils:

> *And God shall wipe away all tears from their eyes; and there shall be no more death, neither sorrow, nor crying, neither shall there be any more pain: for the former things are passed away.* (Rev 21:4)

The earth is sin-cursed because the first two people rejected God's wise counsel. Therefore, even the problems not directly caused by man today were indirectly caused by man. It was Adam who sinned, and we would all do the same; we would act independently from God and disobey Him, because everyone who is less than God will act less than godly. Much of life's suffering continues to be caused by man and is done in opposition to God's will:

> *And GOD saw that the wickedness of man was great in the earth, and that every imagination of the thoughts of his heart was only evil continually. And it repented the LORD that he had made man on the earth, and it grieved him at his heart.* (Gen 6:5-6)

Humanity is fallen and sinful, perpetrating many evils. Consider God's point of view in this matter; He created a wonderful world for mankind, but men do not appreciate it or love each other; instead, they continually sin and rebel against God. It is understandably frustrating when things seem unfair, but the Bible not only reveals a solution to sin; it introduces its readers to a God of ultimate justice; nobody will "get away" with anything:

> *Dearly beloved, avenge not yourselves, but rather give place unto wrath: for it is written, Vengeance is mine; I will repay, saith the Lord.* (Ro 12:19)

The issue of suffering returns us to the matter of God's character, specifically to whether or not He is good. The evidence that He is good can be seen in the hope He offers for our future. The biblical meaning of hope is to have a confident expectation:

For God sent not his Son into the world to condemn the world; but that the world through him might be saved. (Jn 3:17)

But I would not have you to be ignorant, brethren, concerning them which are asleep, that ye sorrow not, even as others which have no hope. (1 Thes 4:13)

Now the God of hope fill you with all joy and peace in believing, that ye may abound in hope, through the power of the Holy Ghost. (Ro 15:13)

In hope of eternal life, which God, that cannot lie, promised before the world began. (Titus 1:2)

Blessed be the God and Father of our Lord Jesus Christ, which according to his abundant mercy hath begotten us again unto a lively hope by the resurrection of Jesus Christ from the dead... (1 Pet 1:3)

Wherefore gird up the loins of your mind, be sober, and hope to the end for the grace that is to be brought unto you at the revelation of Jesus Christ... (1 Pet 1:13)

If you agree that much of what happens in this world is not according to God's will, you may be able to look away from its calamities and find that you can place confidence in the message of the Bible. It claims to tell us who God is, and how to be assured of a perfect eternity with all those who believe His "good news" message, found in 1 Corinthians 15:1-4.

_____

_____

_____

6

"I believe in a god of my own understanding, a higher power, maybe like the 'Star Wars force,' but not the God of the Bible."

That at the name of Jesus every knee should bow, of things in heaven, and things in earth, and things under the earth; And that every tongue should confess that Jesus Christ is Lord, to the glory of God the Father. (Phil 2:10-11)

Many people have developed their own ideas about who God is, just like we, the authors, did before we were Christians. We had no proof of our beliefs, and when confronted with evidence to the contrary, we would not consider it. For this reason, it is not surprising that Jesus said many people are willing to believe anything *except* the truth:

*And **because** I tell you the truth, ye believe me not.* (Jn 8:45)

An impersonal force that can be used to accomplish things is a popular idea about who God is. The "Star Wars force," for example, can be used for good or evil, depending upon who wields it. Nature is a kind of god to some, but nature has no personality; you can't have a relationship with forces of nature. Tribal gods are unpredictable and untrustworthy. Mohammed, the founder of Islam, made his tribal god, Allah, the god of a new religion. But Allah has no concern for his followers. He is distant, unjust, and not at all merciful. His followers cannot count on him and never know what to expect from him. The God of the Bible is both personal and concerned for all mankind.

Despite the different ideas of various religions about who God is, they all teach some standard of behavior and have rules to follow. With a standard comes the need for a judge who must determine if followers have met it. Neither nature nor a "force" can make moral determinations; only a personal god can be a judge. Only a person has a conscience and can know right from wrong. The God of the Bible is more than a judge; He is a righteous judge. He calls mankind to use reason and to display virtue; He even provided us with a comprehensive manual explaining how to do so. The scriptures testify that the character of God is goodness and love, kindness and grace, reason and justice, help and hope. He is a personal God, and Christians believe that we can know Him, trust Him, and have a relationship with Him:

> *And I will give them an heart to know me, that I am the LORD: and they shall be my people, and I will be their God: for they shall return unto me with their whole heart.* (Jer 24:7)

> *But let him that glorieth glory in this, that he understandeth and knoweth me, that I am the LORD which exercise lovingkindness, judgment, and righteousness, in the earth: for in these things I delight, saith the LORD.* (Jer 9:24)

> *Behold, we count them happy which endure. Ye have heard of the patience of Job, and have seen the end of the Lord; that the Lord is very pitiful, and of tender mercy.* (Jas 5:11)

> *This then is the message which we have heard of him, and declare unto you, that God is light, and in him is no darkness at all.* (1 Jn 1:5)

The Bible describes a God who is personal and of upright character. He offers security and assurance to those who believe Him:

> *These things have I written unto you that believe on the name of the Son of God; that ye may **know** that ye have eternal life, and that ye may believe on the name of the Son of God.* (1 Jn 5:13)

Unlike an impersonal force, or a capricious counterfeit deity, the all-powerful God of Christianity says that He knows the future, is involved in it, and brings about the outcomes He desires:

> *I'm telling you this now, before it happens, so that when it does happen, you may believe that I AM.* (Jn 13:19 ISV)

> *Behold, I am the LORD, the God of all flesh: is there anything too hard for me?* (Jer 32:27)

> *Declaring the end from the beginning, and from ancient times the things that are not yet done, saying, My counsel shall stand, and I will do all my pleasure...* (Isa 46:10)

> *For I am the LORD: I will speak, and the word that I shall speak shall come to pass; it shall be no more prolonged: for in your days, O rebellious house, will I say the word, and will perform it, saith the Lord GOD.* (Ezek 12:25)

The God of the Bible says that He has always existed and that He is the only God:

> *Unto thee it was shewed, that thou mightest know that the LORD he is God; there is none else beside him.* (Deut 4:35)

> *Before the mountains were brought forth, or ever thou hadst formed the earth and the world, even from everlasting to everlasting, thou art God.* (Ps 90:2)

> *Ye are my witnesses, saith the LORD, and my servant whom I have chosen: that ye may know and believe me, and*

> *understand that I am he: before me there was no God formed, neither shall there be after me. I, even I, am the LORD; and beside me there is no saviour. I have declared, and have saved, and I have shewed, when there was no strange god among you: therefore ye are my witnesses saith the LORD, that I am God. Yea, before the day was I am he; and there is none that can deliver out of my hand: I will work, and who shall let it?* (Isa 43:10-13)

A force, lacking personhood, cannot give the world spiritual concepts such as beauty, liberty, or love. The competing gods of other religions cannot prove themselves to be the one true God. The God of the Bible says that He is the one and only Creator:

> *Thus saith the LORD, thy redeemer, and he that formed thee from the womb, I am the LORD that maketh all things; that stretcheth forth the heavens alone; that spreadeth abroad the earth by myself...* (Isa 44:24)

> *I have made the earth, and created man upon it: I, even my hands, have stretched out the heavens, and all their host have I commanded.* (Isa 45:12)

> *For thus saith the LORD that created the heavens; God himself that formed the earth and made it; he hath established it, he created it not in vain, he formed it to be inhabited: I am the LORD; and there is none else.* (Isa 45:18)

Considering who God says He is, one of the most wonderful things about Him is that He lets us know that He understands us. He isn't looking to pounce every time we fail. He knows we are frail, and weak, and very much in need of His tender mercy:

The LORD is merciful and gracious, slow to anger, and plenteous in mercy. He will not always chide: neither will he keep his anger for ever. He hath not dealt with us after our sins; nor rewarded us according to our iniquities. For as the heaven is high above the earth, so great is his mercy toward them that fear him. As far as the east is from the west, so far hath he removed our transgressions from us. Like as a father pitieth his children, so the LORD pitieth them that fear him. For he knoweth our frame; he remembereth that we are dust. (Ps 103:8-14)

Unlike the elements of the earth, or some kind of "force," or a distant, unknowable god, the God of the Bible declares that He is the God who saves. No religion in the world or in history can say that its god sacrificed himself to save all mankind. The God of the Bible is a just God and a good God. We hope you will consider the Bible's claim that He really is the true God.

_____

_____

_____

CHAPTER THREE

WHAT HE DID

Death, Burial, and Resurrection for Sin

*Not by works of righteousness which
we have done, but according to his
mercy he saved us...* (Titus 3:5a)

Having examined objections to "who He is" in chapter 2, we now turn our attention to "what He did." Christians believe that Jesus Christ died on a cross as a sacrifice for the sins of the world, taking upon Himself the wrath of God against sin. After He died, He was buried and then rose from the grave, having been victorious over sin and death. His sacrifice as a substitute for mankind makes available, by faith, a spiritual birth and a relationship with God, apart from any human effort, good works, or law. This chapter answers objections to what the Bible says that Jesus accomplished on the cross. Objections to what He did range from denials that it happened to claims that it is not sufficient to save. Some question its universal availability, while others see Christianity as simply a moral lifestyle rather than a payment on a debt that every person owes. We hope you find these Bible verses and brief explanations helpful toward your understanding of the significance of what Jesus did.

It Didn't Happen?

The Bible contains the detailed historical record of the death, burial and resurrection of Jesus Christ, including the fact that there were hundreds of witnesses to it. Although it is a thoroughly documented event of ancient history, some deny it occurred. For example, a studied Muslim or Jew may deny the resurrection because both Islam and modern, non-biblical Judaism dispute the Bible's record of events. In the first case, Islam teaches that Jesus was not crucified:

"That they said (in boast), 'We killed Christ Jesus the son of Mary, the Messenger of Allah';—but they killed him not, nor crucified him, but so it was made to appear to them, and those who differ therein are full of doubts, with no (certain) knowledge, but only conjecture to follow, for of a surety they killed him not." (Koran, Sura 4:157)

Similarly, Judaism denies the resurrection of Christ and does not accept Him as Israel's prophesied savior. Matthew reports in his gospel that in an effort to cover up Jesus' resurrection, the chief priests and elders of Israel bribed the Roman guards to lie about the disappearance of His body:

And when they were assembled with the elders, and had taken counsel, they gave large money unto the soldiers, Saying, Say ye, His disciples came by night, and stole him away while we slept. And if this come to the governor's ears, we will persuade him, and secure you. So they took the money, and did as they were taught: and this saying is commonly reported among the Jews until this day. (Mt 28:12-15)

It Happened, But...

Some who assent to the biblical record of history and its testimony of Jesus' sacrifice may nevertheless disagree that the death of Jesus was a sufficient sacrifice for sin. They believe that something more than faith in the death, burial, and resurrection of Jesus Christ is needed for deliverance from damnation. From the Christian perspective, such a belief is considered "legalism," meaning that human effort, often expressed in religious rules or laws, is also needed. One way to explain the concept of gracious salvation is to use as an example the one man who seems least deserving of it, the universally agreed upon most-evil-person-ever.

7

"So you think anyone can go to heaven? Even Hitler?!"

For there is no respect of persons with God. (Ro 2:11)

Imagine that someone you love has been murdered, and that the penalty for murder is death. The murderer does not want to die, and has asked how he can make it up to you for killing your loved one. Is there anything this person can do in order to make it right? Of course not. Nothing the murderer could ever do would bring that person back, or make it "ok." Now imagine that the murderer asks the judge to send him to a luxury resort instead of death row because other than the one murder, he is "basically a good person." The example seems ridiculous, but most people do think of themselves as "basically good." Because every one of us is continually sinning, we should question the belief which qualifies us for a blissful eternity, but does not afford it to others. I might think I am not as bad as somebody else, but comparisons are irrelevant when everybody is guilty.

Christianity teaches that every person has sinned and offended God. Once a person has committed a sin, it cannot be undone; he cannot "fix" it or make it "ok" that he has sinned. So how then can a person come into a right standing with God when a sin has already been committed? He cannot. This is why salvation *must* be gracious. The one who places his faith for eternity in the Gospel of Christ will gain something he does not deserve; he is given what someone else accomplished on his behalf. This is referred to as "grace through faith." Faith is the perfect way to access grace, because it excludes any kind of human effort, achievement, or personal righteousness. Mighty or weak, genius or average, pious or fallen, any person is able to receive forgiveness of sins…even Hitler.

Perhaps from your perspective, it may seem unfair that an evil person has the same opportunity for salvation as a sweet grandmother, but if fairness was the standard, the Bible declares that we would all be in the lake of fire. Our unworthiness for heaven is not in comparison to others, but in comparison to the perfect holiness of God. God hates sin and cannot allow it in heaven. He not only declares Himself holy, He also says that He is just. The Bible teaches that God has no "respect of persons," meaning He deals with all men justly, and without bias, even Hitler (Ro 2:11, Acts 10:34, Eph 6:9, Col 3:25).

Perhaps it is because we think too well of most people (excepting Hitler), that the offer of salvation to all seems unfair. A few seem so bad that we see ourselves as faring well in comparison. The refrain that "people are basically good," however, contradicts the biblical declaration that we are all born sinners, in need of salvation from sin, and in possession of nothing worthy of God. Children are a familiar example of this; while we often refer to them as "innocent," they do not need to be taught to hit their siblings, hoard their toys, or say, "No!" to Mommy. The assessment of our condition as unworthy sinners is not from our point of view, but from the perfect and holy perspective of God, as expressed by King David:

> Behold, I was shapen in iniquity; and in sin did my mother conceive me. (Ps 51:5)

A person who trusts in his own good works for deliverance from sin's penalty must necessarily believe that he has something of value to offer God. But God excludes human effort for salvation, proclaiming that even our "righteousnesses," our very *best* works, are filthy and tainted with sin:

> But we are all as an unclean thing, and all our righteousnesses are as filthy rags; and we all do fade as a leaf; and our iniquities, like the wind, have taken us away. (Isa 64:6)

If we believe the evaluation described in the Bible, then offering God the "filthy rags" of our so-called goodness seems as ludicrous as the murderer who thinks he deserves a vacation at a luxury resort. Because human good works do not change anything we have done to offend God, we may recognize that we need His mercy to save us. If one believes, however, that "good people" are qualified for heaven, while Hitler and a few others are not, then human merit is the determining factor in salvation, and grace through faith alone has been rejected. Such a view judges the death, burial, and resurrection of Jesus Christ insufficient to save, and is, therefore, incompatible with the Christian Gospel.

Making no meritorious distinctions among men, God's word declares that Jesus Christ died for the sins of the whole world:

> And he is the propitiation for our sins: and not for ours only, but also **for the sins of the whole world.** (1 Jn 2:2)

For God so loved the world, *that he gave his only begotten Son, that whosoever believeth in him should not perish, but have everlasting life. For God sent not his Son into the world to condemn the world; but **that the world through him might be saved**.* (Jn 3:16-17)

*And said unto the woman, Now we believe, not because of thy saying: for we have heard him ourselves, and know that this is indeed the Christ, **the Saviour of the world**.* (Jn 4:42)

*I am the living bread which came down from heaven: if any man eat of this bread, he shall live for ever: and the bread that I will give is my flesh, which **I will give for the life of the world**.* (Jn 6:51)

*To wit, that God was in Christ, **reconciling the world** unto himself, not imputing their trespasses unto them; and hath committed unto us the word of reconciliation.* (2 Cor 5:19)

According to the Bible, Jesus died for the sins of the world because every person needs deliverance from sin. Nothing any one of us can do will rectify our offenses. Only by the grace and mercy of God can we exchange the penalty that we owe for sin with the penalty that Jesus bore on our behalf. The biblical warning is that because many will reject the payment for their sins, the whole world will not be in heaven. Nonetheless, the message of salvation is known as good news: all those who simply believe it will be there, and this offer is available to all.

_____

_____

_____

8

"Yes, I believe the gospel, but I still need to do my share."

> *And whosoever liveth and believeth in me shall never die. Believest thou this?* (Jn 11:26)

There are some who voice agreement with the Gospel of Christ, but upon detailed discussion are actually at odds with it because they believe that they need to contribute to their own salvation. The New Testament of the Bible is written to Christians, and Christians are called to help one another and to share the Gospel with non-Christians. This call to do good works *after* salvation may be confused with and combined with the Gospel. Because God allows the members of His body, the Church, to share in His work here on earth, a person may see no problem with "doing his part" in salvation as well. Man's partnership with God, however, is only after being cleansed by the blood of Christ, through His sacrifice on the cross.

A person who adds his efforts to those of Christ is unlikely to consider himself a co-redeemer, but this is the unavoidable conclusion if he must contribute to his own salvation. The Bible teaches that we are to simply believe in order to receive the gift of salvation:

> *To him give all the prophets witness, that through his name whosoever believeth in him shall receive remission of sins.* (Acts 10:43)

> *For the wages of sin is death; but the gift of God is eternal life through Jesus Christ our Lord.* (Ro 6:23)

> *But God, who is rich in mercy, for his great love wherewith he loved us, Even when we were dead in sins, hath quickened us together with Christ, (by grace ye are saved;) And hath raised us up together, and made us sit together in heavenly places in Christ Jesus: That in the ages to come he might shew the exceeding riches of his grace in his kindness toward us through Christ Jesus. For by grace are ye saved through faith; and that not of yourselves: it is the **gift** of God: **Not of works**, lest any man should boast.* (Eph 2:4-9)

Christians are privileged to share in God's work of proclaiming the good news of salvation from sins. Their own faith in the Gospel, however, must precede this partnership. The Bible teaches that to work for salvation in any way is to reject the grace which has been provided by God. You may be very well-intentioned if you are one who wants to pitch in and do your share in salvation. We hope it is clear that gracious salvation is only gracious if it is not earned. A gift must be freely given. To work for something is to reject it as a gift, and because no person can make up for having sinned against God, there is no work that can be done anyway. The Bible calls every person to believe the Gospel of Christ for salvation, the good news message found in 1 Corinthians 15:1-4.

_____

_____

_____

9

"So you just throw out part of the Bible? I believe all of it!"

> *For whatsoever things were written aforetime were written for our learning, that we through patience and comfort of the scriptures might have hope.* (Ro 15:4)

Closely related to the previous objections is the specific belief in the need to practice the Law of Moses, also known as the Mosaic Law, as part of salvation. Objections of this sort may be held by people who believe and respect the Bible, but who erroneously conclude that all of the Bible is currently applicable. The Bible teaches that God administered the Nation of Israel by law, but administers the church by the principle of grace. In either case, salvation is by faith. The addition of Old Testament practices to the Gospel is known as "legalism," a term which refers to the addition of religious laws as a requirement for salvation.

Christianity teaches that salvation is gracious, meaning it is given freely and accessed by nothing more than faith in the Gospel message. If law-works are needed for salvation, then Jesus' sacrifice did not fully pay for sin. Jesus proclaimed on the cross, "It is finished," because His payment for sin was satisfactory and had been accepted by God the Father (Jn 19:30).

> *Take heed therefore unto yourselves, and to all the flock, over the which the Holy Ghost hath made you overseers, to feed the church of God, which he hath purchased with his own blood.* (Acts 20:28)

The previous verse makes reference to a completed purchase. It is helpful to think of sin as a debt, and of Christ's death as the payment that satisfies it. If you were to pay your car loan, that debt is gone. Similarly, if Jesus pays my sin debt, it too is gone. But, if I am doing works to please, appease, or pay God, I am in fact offering those works as a payment for my sins, instead of accepting the gift of salvation. It cannot be both. Either something is a gift, or it is worked for and earned or purchased. Any payment makes an item received no longer a gift. Believing that the salvation purchased by Christ must be gained or earned by the sinner means that either the gift has been rejected, or the offer has not been understood. God is not impressed with our works; He is impressed with the work of the Son. According to the Bible, anyone who rejects the payment of Jesus Christ for his sins will spend eternity in the lake of fire, paying for his own sins (Rev 20:14-15). Because Christians believe this, we preach the Gospel of Christ to each who will hear.

No Defense for Law

The objection that Christians have thrown out the Old Testament is a serious charge which deserves additional examination. Numerous Bible verses specifically exclude law-works for salvation. It is not a rejection of the Old Testament to believe that Jesus' death paid for all sin without the works of the Law. The Old Testament scriptures did have a purpose in regard to the arrival of the prophesied Messiah: they pointed man to his need for a savior and identified the Savior when He arrived.

> *Therefore by the deeds of the law there shall no flesh be justified in his sight: for by the law is the knowledge of sin.* (Ro 3:20)

> And I knew him not: but that he should be made manifest to
> Israel, therefore am I come baptizing with water. (Jo 1:31)

The Old Testament remains important today. Its testimony of the love, faithfulness, and longsuffering of God as He dealt with His chosen nation, Israel, is instructive and comforting to Christians:

> For whatsoever things were written aforetime were written for our learning, that we through patience and comfort of the scriptures might have hope. (Ro 15:4)

The New Testament teaches that salvation is gracious and accessed by faith, not by law. Law-keeping cannot be comingled with salvation because doing so is a denial of the sufficiency of Christ's payment for sin. Additionally, it is absolutely impossible for anyone to keep even a fraction of the Law, which had 613 requirements. No person alive can even keep the most well-known 10, and the same is true for any law system; no matter what rules any of us might set for ourselves, eventually we will break them.

The Law of Moses expressed God's *perfect* standard. Therefore, any lesser level of performance in an effort to gain salvation has already fallen short. No one but Jesus Christ ever kept the law, so if it is needed for entrance into heaven, nobody is getting in.

> For neither they themselves who are circumcised keep the law; but desire to have you circumcised, that they may glory in your flesh. (Gal 6:13)

> Now therefore why tempt ye God, to put a yoke upon the neck of the disciples, which neither our fathers nor we were able to bear? (Acts 15:10)

Another problem with adding law requirements to salvation is that the law cannot save and *was never intended to*. Its purpose was to reveal sin and to show those who lived under it their need for a savior. Laws do nothing more than inform a lawbreaker of his violation; they cannot deliver the lawbreaker from its penalty. For example, if I drive past a 35 mph speed limit sign while driving 55, it shows me that I am guilty. Obeying the law in the future does not change the fact that I broke it in the past, nor does it exonerate me from its consequences.

> *But now **we are delivered from the law**, that being dead wherein we were held; that we should serve in newness of spirit, and not in the oldness of the letter. What shall we say then? Is the law sin? God forbid. Nay, **I had not known sin, but by the law**: for I had not known lust, except the law had said, Thou shalt not covet.* (Ro 7:6-7)

> *For **the law made nothing perfect**, but the bringing in of a better hope did; by the which we draw nigh unto God.* (Heb 7:19)

> *For **the law** having a shadow of good things to come, and not the very image of the things, **can never with those sacrifices** which they offered year by year continually **make the comers thereunto perfect.*** (Heb 10:1)

> *Wherefore the law was our schoolmaster to bring us unto Christ, that we might be justified by faith. But **after that faith is come, we are no longer under a schoolmaster**.* (Gal 3:24-25)

> *For **what the law could not do**, in that it was weak through the flesh, God sending his own Son in the likeness of sinful flesh, and for sin, condemned sin in the flesh...* (Ro 8:3)

Because God saves by grace through faith and not by a system of laws, adding law requirements actually undermines the Gospel, forcing the law-keeper to reject grace in order to put himself under rule of law:

I do not frustrate the grace of God: for if righteousness come by the law, then Christ is dead in vain. (Gal 2:21)

The sting of death is sin; and the strength of sin is the law. (1 Cor 15:56)

The practice of law-works is the opposite of accepting God's grace by faith. They are wholly incompatible:

And if by grace, then is it no more of works: otherwise grace is no more grace. But if it be of works, then is it no more grace: otherwise work is no more work. (Ro 11:6)

Where is boasting then? It is excluded. By what law? of works? Nay: but by the law (principle) *of faith. Therefore we conclude that a man is justified by faith without the deeds of the law.* (Ro 3:27-28, clarification added)

For if Abraham were justified by works, he hath whereof to glory; but not before God. For what saith the scripture? Abraham believed God, and it was counted unto him for righteousness. Now to him that worketh is the reward not reckoned of grace, but of debt. But to him that worketh not, but believeth on him that justifieth the ungodly, his faith is counted for righteousness. Even as David also describeth the blessedness of the man, unto whom God imputeth righteousness without works, Saying, Blessed are they whose iniquities are forgiven, and whose sins are covered. Blessed is the man to whom the Lord will not impute sin. (Ro 4:2-8)

> *Nevertheless knowing that a man is not justified by the works of the Law but through faith in Christ Jesus, even we have believed in Christ Jesus, so that we may be justified by faith in Christ and not by the works of the Law; since by the works of the Law no flesh will be justified.* (Gal 2:16, NASB)

The justification of the believer before God is by faith in Jesus Christ, not by works. The testimony of scripture is also clear that the administration of the church is by grace, not by the Mosaic Law:

> *For sin shall not have dominion over you: for ye are not under the law, but under grace.* (Ro 6:14)

> *But if ye be led of the Spirit, ye are not under the law.* (Gal 5:18)

> *Be not thou therefore ashamed of the testimony of our Lord, nor of me his prisoner: but be thou partaker of the afflictions of the gospel according to the power of God; Who hath saved us, and called us with an holy calling, not according to our works, but according to his own purpose and grace, which was given us in Christ Jesus before the world began, But is now made manifest by the appearing of our Saviour Jesus Christ, who hath abolished death, and hath brought life and immortality to light through the gospel...* (2 Tim 1:8-10)

Adding to the hopelessness of law-keeping is that nobody can honestly claim to keep the Law, which included temple sacrifices and stonings, for example. A person who claims to keep the Law can only select parts of Israel's law to follow. But the Law is one entity, a complete and indivisible package, representing God's holiness. Breaking any part of it breaks His entire Law, and performing only part of it does not qualify as keeping the Law. Trying to keep some fragment of the Law is a futile religious exercise.

For whosoever shall keep the whole law, and yet offend in one point, he is guilty of all. (Jas 2:10)

For as many as are of the works of the law are under the curse: for it is written Cursed is every one that continueth not in all things which are written in the book of the law to do them. But that no man is justified by the law in the sight of God, it is evident: for, The just shall live by faith. And the law is not of faith: but, The man that doeth them shall live in them. Christ hath redeemed us from the curse of the law, being made a curse for us: for it is written, Cursed is every one that hangeth on a tree... (Gal 3:10-13)

For I testify again to every man that is circumcised, that he is a debtor to do the whole law. Christ is become of no effect unto you, whosoever of you are justified by the law; ye are fallen from grace. (Gal 5:3-4)

For Christ is the end of the law for righteousness to every one that believeth. For Moses describeth the righteousness which is of the law, That the man which doeth those things shall live by them. (Ro 10:4-5)

Christians are not throwing out the Old Testament by not keeping the Law. We recognize that the Law had its role, as did the Garden of Eden, Noah's ark, Solomon's temple, and many other things that are not part of God's current program. We see the Law for what it was and live by grace through faith, a vastly superior program given to administer the body of Christ, the Church (Heb 7:19, 7:22, 8:6).

_____

_____

_____

10

"I do my best and try to be a good person. I've lived a pretty good life, never cheated on my wife, or used drugs, or killed anyone. I sure don't live like so-and-so. I don't think I'm that bad that I deserve to burn in hell!"

Closely related to the belief that some folks are too evil to be saved is the commonly held belief in one's own relative goodness. Every person alive might claim to be morally superior to someone else in one way or another, but the belief in personal goodness for salvation is not consistent with biblical teaching. What it fails to acknowledge is that God's evaluation of each of us is the relevant measurement of goodness. The Bible teaches that it is *God's* standard, not ours, that will determine our eternal destiny. It also warns that all men are sinners and that judgment day will someday arrive. According to the Bible, mankind lacks the righteousness needed to enter into God's presence, and therefore, all who refuse the righteousness offered by Christ will be separated from God forever:

> *What then? are we better than they? No, in no wise: for we have before proved both Jews and Gentiles, that they are all under sin; As it is written, There is none righteous, no, not one: There is none that understandeth, there is none that seeketh after God. They are all gone out of the way, they are together become unprofitable; there is none that doeth good, no, not one. Their throat is an open sepulchre; with their tongues they have used deceit; the poison of asps is under their lips: Whose mouth is full of cursing and bitterness: Their feet are swift to shed blood: Destruction and misery are in their ways: And the way of peace have they not known: There is no*

fear of God before their eyes. Now we know that what things soever the law saith, it saith to them who are under the law: that every mouth may be stopped, and all the world may become guilty before God. Therefore by the deeds of the law there shall no flesh be justified in his sight: for by the law is the knowledge of sin. But now the righteousness of God without the law is manifested, being witnessed by the law and the prophets; Even the righteousness of God which is by faith of Jesus Christ unto all and upon all them that believe: for there is no difference: For all have sinned, and come short of the glory of God; Being justified freely by his grace through the redemption that is in Christ Jesus: Whom God hath set forth to be a propitiation through faith in his blood, to declare his righteousness for the remission of sins that are past, through the forbearance of God; To declare, I say, at this time his righteousness: that he might be just, and the justifier of him which believeth in Jesus. (Ro 3:9-26; see also Ps 14:1-3, 53:1-3)

And I saw the dead, small and great, stand before God; and the books were opened: and another book was opened, which is the book of life: and the dead were judged out of those things which were written in the books, according to their works. And the sea gave up the dead which were in it; and death and hell delivered up the dead which were in them: and they were judged every man according to their works. And death and hell were cast into the lake of fire. This is the second death. And whosoever was not found written in the book of life was cast into the lake of fire. (Rev 20:12-15)

Because God hates sin, and heaven would not be heavenly with sinners in it, one must be cleansed of sin to enter. This is accomplished in a person when he accepts the death, burial, and resurrection of Jesus Christ on behalf of his sins. The Christian belief is that only by this method can one enter into the presence of God (Jn 16:8-11).

___

___

___

11

"I've been a Christian my whole life. I was born in a Christian home, I was baptized and confirmed, I go to church, pray, and have even read the whole Bible. I am offended that you would bring up salvation!"

For Christ sent me not to baptize, but to preach the gospel: not with wisdom of words, lest the cross of Christ should be made of none effect. (1 Cor 1:17)

Anyone can call himself a Christian, but biblically speaking, the term only applies to those who have come to faith in the Gospel of Christ, the salvation message found in 1 Corinthians 15:1-4. A person who is devoted to religious observance, for example, is not necessarily "born again," the spiritual condition that results from faith in the Gospel. Activities such as water baptism, confirmation, or church attendance do not make one a Christian. Neither is anyone "born" a Christian or counted by God to be a Christian through family or cultural affiliation. Superior lifestyle choices, church attendance, Bible reading, the observance of sacraments, and other externals—however sincerely practiced—have no bearing on the spiritual birth needed to enter into a relationship with God.

> *Jesus answered and said unto him, Verily, verily, I say unto thee, Except a man be born again, he cannot see the kingdom of God. ... Marvel not that I said unto thee, Ye must be born again.* (Jo 3:3, 7)

> *Being born again, not of corruptible seed, but of incorruptible, by the word of God, which liveth and abideth for ever.* (1 Pet 1:23)

If one's faith is in one's religious practices, it is not in the finished work of Jesus Christ on the cross for sins. As explained in Chapter One, the spiritual birth is what defines a Christian, and that birth is by faith in the Gospel message of 1 Corinthians 15:1-4.

12

"What about all the good things I have done? I think I have done more good than evil. In the end, I think my good deeds will outweigh my bad deeds."

> *Not by works of righteousness which we have done, but according to his mercy he saved us, by the washing of regeneration, and renewing of the Holy Ghost...* (Titus 3:5)

Imagining the deeds of one's life on a scale of balance, with good works on one side and sins on the other, is a common way of estimating the likelihood of being rescued from eternal damnation. According to the Bible, however, what a person needs to do instead is to compare his good works to those of Jesus Christ. The perfect, sinless life and sacrificial death of Jesus is the standard against which we will be compared on judgment day. It may seem reasonable to think that God's judgment will be similar to a statue of Lady Justice in a courtroom, who holds a balance in her hand. But there is a problem with the analogy: Lady Justice is not comparing good deeds to bad deeds; she is weighing evidence! This begs the question, "Is there evidence that I am a sinner?"

The Bible contains nothing to support the idea that one can do a certain number of "bad deeds" as long as a greater amount of good is done. Far from accepting a certain amount of sin, God, the perfect judge, is holy and is offended by all sin. Only a corrupt judge would exonerate a man for murder because he once saved someone's life. To think that Almighty God would implement such a system is not reasonable, because a system that balances good deeds against bad is allowing those bad deeds and deeming them permissible, as long as they are "balanced with good."

On the practical side, how many "good deeds" does a person ever really do? Most of the things that people do are out of necessity and self-interest. Meeting obligations, obeying laws, and fulfilling agreements can hardly be characterized as "good deeds." Some religions count every prayer as a good deed, but for what do most people pray? Are most of the world's prayers for wants and wishes? How many plead as David did to do nothing but the will of God (Ps 143:10)? Relying upon an accumulation of good deeds for salvation is to trust in one's own achievements rather than in the death, burial, and resurrection of Jesus Christ for the sins of the world. According to the Bible, however, each person must be convinced that the Gospel of Christ, found in 1 Corinthians 15:1-4, is true and sufficient to save.

_____

_____

_____

13

"I don't agree with you; I have my own beliefs."
"I sincerely believe in the religion I practice, and I think God will honor that."

Sanctify them through thy truth: thy word is truth. (Jn 17:17)

Some objections to what Jesus did come from the view that nearly any religious belief is valid, and that Jesus' ministry was not unique. For the person who has his own beliefs or feels comfortable in the religion of his choice, "sincerity" is often used as the standard and measure of faith. According to the Bible, however, it is truth and not sincerity that matters to God. The Bible defines itself as the very truth, the singular revelation of God Himself. If this is so, will God then bow to whatever religion a person wishes to practice? Can a man put himself in God's place, expecting God to be submissive to his religious idea or plan? Is the biblical offer of Jesus' sacrifice for sin of no greater value than any religious notion? These are questions which might be worthy of consideration. What might also be worthwhile is some investigation into whether or not there is any evidence of the religious beliefs one holds. Here are some examples of the truth claims of the Bible:

Jesus saith unto him, I am the way, the truth, and the life: no man cometh unto the Father, but by me. (Jn 14:6)

And ye shall know the truth, and the truth shall make you free. (Jn 8:32)

And this is life eternal, that they might know thee the only true God, and Jesus Christ, whom thou hast sent. (Jn 17:3)

And for their sakes I sanctify myself, that they also might be sanctified through the truth. (Jn 17:19)

In whom ye also trusted, after that ye heard the word of truth, the gospel of your salvation: in whom also after that ye believed, ye were sealed with that holy Spirit of promise. (Eph 1:13)

For the hope which is laid up for you in heaven, whereof ye heard before in the word of the truth of the gospel. (Col 1:5)

For this cause also thank we God without ceasing, because, when ye received the word of God which ye heard of us, ye received it not as the word of men, but as it is in truth, the word of God, which effectually worketh also in you that believe. (1 Thes 2:13)

But we are bound to give thanks alway to God for you, brethren beloved of the Lord, because God hath from the beginning chosen you to salvation through sanctification of the Spirit and belief of the truth... (2 Thes 2:13)

Who will have all men to be saved, and to come unto the knowledge of the truth. (1 Tim 2:4)

But if I tarry long, that thou mayest know how thou oughtest to behave thyself in the house of God, which is the church of the living God, the pillar and ground of the truth. (1 Tim 3:15)

To see the truth means to see things as they really are. Christians believe that only God can see the truth of all things; for that reason, we need His word to teach us what is true. A person can be sincere and yet be wrong. Regardless of one's sincerity in believing something, when the issue is eternity, only that which is true is of value. It is up to each individual to decide if he will consider the testimony of the Bible to be truthful.

_____

_____

_____

CHAPTER FOUR

WHY I NEED IT

For Sin

It is a fearful thing to fall into the hands of the living God. (Heb 10:31)

Objections to the Gospel of Christ are commonly about specific teachings, but they may also be due to disinterest or a lack of concern about issues related to religion. Some people find matters of faith to be foolish or a waste of time; they may not believe in an afterlife or in the idea of justice in the end. Others believe they are already "good with God." The Bible teaches that all men are sinners, and that our sinful condition has separated them from God. Man is accountable to his creator, and his sins must be dealt with. This is the "why" of the Gospel. If you hold views which cause you to doubt the Christian message, perhaps one of the following examples will lead you to consider whether a solution to the universal problem of sin is something that each of us needs.

14

"What is someone dying on a cross going to do for me? Religion is for other people, and a crutch for the weak. I don't need saving."

> *He has fixed a day in which He will judge the world in righteousness through a Man whom He has appointed, having furnished proof to all men by raising Him from the dead.*
> (Acts 17:31 NASB)

An old saying for going to jail or prison is to describe the convict as "paying a debt to society." The phrase recognizes that when someone commits a crime, he has harmed his community or a member of it. Since the criminal cannot undo what has been done, he must pay for his crime in some way, such as with a fine, imprisonment, or even with his life. According to the Bible, committing a sin also creates a debt, but with God.

> *Against thee, thee only, have I sinned, and done this evil in thy sight: that thou mightest be justified when thou speakest, and be clear when thou judgest.* (Ps 51:4)

Even though it varies somewhat across time, and cultures, and among individuals, each person has an innate sense of right and wrong. Most of us would readily agree that we have committed many wrongs during our lifetime. We would also affirm that we obey rules, discipline our children, and use the justice system. Christians believe that these ordinary facts of life support the biblical teaching that we each have a conscience, and that we will one day be accountable to God for our actions. Denying this is sometimes due to the desire to avoid accountability. According to the Bible, man not only sins, but is a sinner by nature, meaning that he is a sinner from birth. Rebellion against God is the hallmark of sin, and the Bible warns that there is a consequence for sin.

> *Behold, I was shapen in iniquity; and in sin did my mother conceive me.* (Ps 51:5)

> *But we are all as an unclean thing, and all our righteousnesses are as filthy rags; and we all do fade as a leaf; and our iniquities, like the wind, have taken us away.* (Isa 64:6)

> *And Jesus said unto him, Why callest thou me good? there is none good but one, that is, God.* (Mk 10:18; see also Mt 19:17; Lk 18:19)

> *For the wages of sin is death; but the gift of God is eternal life through Jesus Christ our Lord.* (Ro 6:23)

> *Therefore you have no excuse, everyone of you who passes judgment, for in that which you judge another, you condemn yourself; for you who judge practice the same things. And we know that the judgment of God rightly falls upon those who practice such things. But do you suppose this, O man, when you pass judgment on those who practice such things and do the same yourself, that you will escape the judgment of God? Or do you think lightly of the riches of His kindness and tolerance and patience, not knowing that the kindness of God leads you to repentance? But because of your stubbornness and unrepentant heart you are storing up wrath for yourself in the day of wrath and revelation of the righteous judgment of God, who will render to each person according to his deeds: to those who by perseverance in doing good seek for glory and honor and immortality, eternal life; but to those*

who are selfishly ambitious and do not obey the truth, but obey unrighteousness, wrath and indignation. There will be tribulation and distress for every soul of man who does evil, of the Jew first and also of the Greek, but glory and honor and peace to everyone who does good, to the Jew first and also to the Greek. For there is no partiality with God. ...on the day when, according to my gospel, God will judge the secrets of men through Christ Jesus. (Rom 2:1-11, 16 NASB)

Although people tend to think of themselves in general as "basically good," the Bible says that each of us is tainted by sin in all we desire, think, say, and do. God's conclusion regarding mankind's so-called "goodness" is, "There is none that does good, there is not even one" (Ro 3:12b NASB). Using that standard, then anyone who is not as good as God is not qualified for heaven, and nothing he produces is good enough either. Therefore, every one of us is in need of a solution that only God can provide. If the Bible is correct, then denial is a stall, but not a solution. It warns that one day we will each face God and be held to account for all we have said and done:

So then every one of us shall give account of himself to God. (Ro 14:12)

Nothing in all creation is hidden from God's sight. Everything is uncovered and laid bare before the eyes of him to whom we must give account. (Heb 4:13 NIV)

Not every person who sees no need for Christian salvation, however, denies moral failure. Many will readily acknowledge that they fail in many ways, yet why they need salvation is not apparent to them. This could be due to a lack of understanding or appreciation for what was accomplished on the cross. It is true that many people have died on a cross; perhaps Jesus' death does not seem special, but this unique death fulfilled more than two dozen biblical prophecies. That fact alone is one which you may find worthy of further study.

It is God who chose crucifixion for the Savior's death. The Bible does not explain why a cross was used, but perhaps the horrific nature of this manner of death was intended to portray the seriousness of sin. We are told that under the Law, dying on a tree displayed that the person was cursed by God:

> *Christ hath redeemed us from the curse of the law, being made a curse for us: for it is written, Cursed is every one that hangeth on a tree…* (Gal 3:13)

> *And if a man have committed a sin worthy of death, and he be to be put to death, and thou hang him on a tree: His body shall not remain all night upon the tree, but thou shalt in any wise bury him that day; (for he that is hanged is accursed of God;) that thy land be not defiled, which the LORD thy God giveth thee for an inheritance.* (Deut 21:22-23)

Christians view sin as a curse upon mankind, and the death of our Savior provided release from that curse for all who believe the Gospel of Christ. Therefore, the calling of Christians is to proclaim that of which we are convinced: that faith in Jesus' sacrifice provides the deliverance from sin that every person needs. If you do not see the value in Christianity, or any reason why you need what Jesus offers, we hope that you will at least consider that there is hope for justice in the end, and a loving judge who wants you to be on the right side of justice.

Each person must decide for himself whether he believes the Gospel of Christ, the message revealing God's solution to the problem of sin. You may feel that "religion" is not for you, but if you acknowledge that you have offended God, perhaps it is worth considering the Bible's warning that Jesus Christ is needed to pay for sins. If not, according to the Bible, there is an alternative: each who rejects God's solution to sin will be separated from God forever, bearing the punishment for his own sins in the lake of fire:

> *And the devil that deceived them was cast into the lake of fire and brimstone, where the beast and the false prophet are, and shall be tormented day and night for ever and ever. And I saw a great white throne, and him that sat on it, from whose face the earth and the heaven fled away; and there was found no place for them. And I saw the dead, small and great, stand before God; and the books were opened: and another book was opened, which is the book of life: and the dead were judged out of those things which were written in the books, according to their works. And the sea gave up the dead which were in it; and death and hell delivered up the dead which were in them: and they were judged every man according to their works. And death and hell were cast into the lake of fire. This is the second death. And whosoever was not found written in the book of life was cast into the lake of fire.* (Rev 20:10-15)

Avoiding the lake of fire seems like a good reason to consider salvation. Jesus said that He gave Himself as the object of God's wrath against sin, taking mankind's punishment and dying in our place. Upon believing the Gospel, a sinner is credited with the payment for sin made by Jesus Christ on his behalf. That payment satisfied both the justice and the love of God; the sin debt is justly satisfied, and the sinner is lovingly released from the debt. Free from the guilt for his sins, the one who has believed the Gospel is fit for communion with God, now and into eternity. This is the Christian promise.

___

___

___

15

"My lifestyle is not a sin. God made me this way. Why should I believe a religion that says that I am not okay the way I am?"

...be ye reconciled to God. (2 Cor 5:20b)

As a culture, our interest in religion increasingly comes more from a consumer's viewpoint than from a sinner's. "What will it do for me?" is the mantra of our day, and many who once agreed with the Bible regarding what is sinful now embrace those very acts. One might think that the consumer mindset would welcome the vast benefits of Christian salvation, but it is not so. Many have rejected the biblical pronouncement that mankind is sinful and instead stand in judgment of God for *His* disagreement with *their* views. This position is sometimes coupled with claims that some sins are traits which existed from birth, an issue which matters no more than whether a person was born with any other preference. A person's preferences have no bearing on whether or not God expects and deserves to be believed and obeyed. The Bible's declaration that we are sinners from birth actually supports the idea that some sins develop early in life. Disobedience toward parents, for example, does not take long to develop in children.

From a biblical perspective, when our preferences develop is a non-issue. What matters in regard to the Christian faith is the difference between what we do and who we are. Regardless of what we do or don't do in terms of sin, who we are in God's eyes is described in the Bible with one word: sinners. Each man's nature leads him to seek or deny his preferences, indulging or suppressing them to varying degrees, depending upon his willpower and convictions. If God asks us to do or not to do something, it follows that we are capable of obeying the request. Because God is love (1 Jn 4:8), we can further conclude that His requests are in our best interest.

Regardless of one's opinion of how we each came to be who we are, the God of the Bible asks man to live according to His will and does not give special exception to any group of people or category of behavior. An individual's own nature, preferences, will, or desires provide no excuse before God. If one denies his need for salvation from sin, the Bible teaches that God may allow him to follow his sinful behaviors to their various consequences:

> *Because that which may be known of God is manifest in them; for God hath shewed it unto them. For the invisible things of him from the creation of the world are clearly seen, being understood by the things that are made, even his eternal power and Godhead; so that they are without excuse: Because that, when they knew God, they glorified him not as God, neither were thankful; but became vain in their*

> *imaginations, and their foolish heart was darkened. ...And even as they did not like to retain God in their knowledge, God gave them over to a reprobate mind, to do those things which are not convenient; Being filled with all unrighteousness, fornication, wickedness, covetousness, maliciousness; full of envy, murder, debate, deceit, malignity; whisperers, Backbiters, haters of God, despiteful, proud, boasters, inventors of evil things, disobedient to parents, Without understanding, covenantbreakers, without natural affection, implacable, unmerciful: Who knowing the judgment of God, that they which commit such things are worthy of death, not only do the same, but have pleasure in them that do them.* (Ro 1:19-21, 28-32)

From the Christian perspective, rejecting the Gospel is an avoidance of the real issue, which is sin. If you take the Bible's word that God does not approve of every whim and desire of mankind, you might also accept its promise that the power of grace provides freedom from sin's power. A holy God has standards, including one way of salvation. A powerful God provides deliverance from the things He asks us not to do. A loving God provides the needed solution freely, found in 1 Corinthians 15:1-4.

_____

_____

_____

16

"I make mistakes, but I wouldn't call myself a sinner."

For all have sinned and fall short of the glory of God.
(Ro 3:23, NASB)

This objection to why one needs salvation begs the question, "What makes someone a sinner?" The biblical definition of sin is to "miss the mark" and "fall short of the glory of God." Most of us could probably agree that we do not have far to fall to be described as "falling short of glory!" God is perfect, and He is offended by sin; humanity is indebted to God for disobeying Him. Jesus paid the debt to God that sinners owe by taking the punishment for sin upon Himself on the cross. This is the "why" of the Gospel.

A common misunderstanding of sin is that being a sinner means that a person is "really bad" or does horrifically evil deeds. Some divide wrongs into seemingly harmless categories such as "little white lies," but the Bible does not. In The Revelation of Jesus Christ to the Apostle John, we see that liars are headed for the lake of fire right along with murderers. The point is that for God, sin is sin. All sin separates us from Him because God is holy.

But the fearful, and unbelieving, and the abominable, and murderers, and whoremongers, and sorcerers, and idolaters, and all liars, shall have their part in the lake which burneth with fire and brimstone: which is the second death. (Rev 21:8)

These six things doth the LORD hate: yea, seven are an abomination unto him: A proud look, a lying tongue, and hands that shed innocent blood, An heart that deviseth wicked imaginations, feet that be swift in running to mischief,

> *A false witness that speaketh lies, and he that soweth discord among brethren.* (Prov 6:16-19)

> *… for whatsoever is not of faith is sin.* (Ro 14:23b)

Adam and Eve in the garden of Eden are good examples of the principle that to sin is simply to fall short of a standard. Adam's sin was the worst sin in the history of mankind, bringing humanity from perfection to a cursed world, from innocence to a knowledge of evil, and from bliss to pain. Eating a piece of off-limits fruit would not typically be considered a horrific act; it was acting independently from God which made it so. God cursed the entire earth for one sin, so comparing God's evaluation of sin to one's own might lead to a reconsideration of what makes someone a sinner. Sin doesn't just mean evil; it can be anything that is not according to God's will. If we are to believe the Bible, each of us is a sinner, and sinners need a savior.

17

"I'll worry about getting saved later, sometime before I die."

> *… now is the accepted time; behold, now is the day of salvation.* (2 Cor 6:2b)

The Bible proclaims that all men are sinners in need of salvation from sin. Procrastination is another way of objecting to the Gospel.

This, however, is a flawed plan, because none of us knows how much time we have on earth, or whether we will have an opportunity to make a lucid decision on our deathbed. If this is your response to the Gospel, we ask you to please reconsider it now. If you are willing to learn some things about it now, you will have some information that you might be glad to have when that day comes.

> *Yet you do not know what your life will be like tomorrow. You are just a vapor that appears for a little while and then vanishes away.* (Jas 4:14 NASB)

> *Like as a father pitieth his children, so the LORD pitieth them that fear him. For he knoweth our frame; he remembereth that we are dust. As for man, his days are as grass: as a flower of the field, so he flourisheth. For the wind passeth over it, and it is gone; and the place thereof shall know it no more.* (Ps 103:13-16)

18

"I'm already a Christian. I just don't believe _____."

Sanctify them through thy truth: thy word is truth. (Jn 17:17)

The Gospel of Christ contains elements which we have labeled who, what, why, how, and where. Who Jesus is, what He did, why we need it, and how we get it are the four elements which comprise the object of faith for salvation in Christianity. While not all Christians agree on every item in the enormous canon of scripture, there are doctrines which are foundational to the faith; rejecting them undermines the overall message of Christianity. For example, if someone denies hell, he believes there is no eternal penalty for sin. The problem with this view is that if there is no penalty, then there is nothing to be saved from and, therefore, no need for a savior. Without the Savior, there is no Christianity, because the object of the Christian faith is Christianity's Savior and what He did. This example illustrates the importance of understanding and believing every part of the Gospel. Following an objection to its logical conclusion exposes the problem caused by excluding a particular doctrine from Christian teaching.

Such an objection leads to another question. Why would a person consider himself a Christian and yet disbelieve the testimony of its scripture? The fifth element within the Gospel of Christ is stated twice: "according to the scriptures." As described in Chapter One, the spiritual birth that defines Christianity is a product of faith. A person may agree with some parts of the Gospel, but may not realize that by rejecting other parts of it, he is rejecting it as a whole. Disbelief in some biblical teachings could prevent a person from the spiritual birth that is needed for a relationship with God. If you find that you believe some parts of the Gospel and not others, please read Chapters One and Six which address the need for a spiritual birth and the importance of believing the testimony of the Bible.

19

"I don't need Jesus. There is nothing after death, just lights out."

For when the Gentiles, which have not the law, do by nature the things contained in the law, these, having not the law, are a law unto themselves: Which shew the work of the law written in their hearts, their conscience also bearing witness, and their thoughts the mean while accusing or else excusing one another... (Ro 2:14-15)

The Gospel of Christ indirectly tells us why we need it: Jesus died on the cross for sins because all men are sinners who need deliverance from sin's penalty and power. But not everyone agrees that there is an afterlife to be saved from or delivered to. A denial of one's need of salvation is sometimes coupled with the atheistic view that man is only a material being and that there is nothing beyond this world. If there is no heaven or hell, there is no need to be saved from hell. While denying God, who is the source of morality and conscience, a believer in atheism probably raises his children using rules of right and wrong. He probably feels badly when he hurts someone, and likes to see justice done when someone is mistreated. Matter cannot create the concepts of right and wrong, nor can it produce any other spiritual concept, such as liberty, beauty, or happiness. The existence of spiritual things is evidence that we are more than material beings. Exposing the contradiction between denying the existence of spiritual life while living by its principles can reveal that there is more to human existence than what we see.

Another problem with the notion of man as material only is that it makes life completely pointless. For example, if death is just "lights out," why should any person bother acting rightly? If there is no judgment at the end, maybe we should stop trying so hard for a "better world" and relax a little. Doing more of what we want might be a better option than trying to follow all the world's rules. We can do good all our lives, but in a generation or two most of us are forgotten anyway; most of our lives don't amount to much, and then we don't exist anymore.

But most people do not believe that we no longer exist after death, nor that our lives and actions do not matter. Most believe that how we raise our children, our faithfulness in marriage, and our honesty at work all have greater meaning than just the earthly rewards for doing so. Many people would even say that their hope of heaven is what gets them through the hard times on earth. The idea that there is nothing beyond this life could make human existence and its sorrows too difficult to bear. Is heaven just a fairy tale to help us get through the day?

There are earthly reasons to do rightly, even if there were no heaven. Some would assert that the source of good behavior is simply the fact that doing rightly makes the world more enjoyable while we are here. It is true that morality improves life on earth. But the supposition that morality is merely a human invention does not explain the broad agreement among people, across the world, and throughout history, as to what constitutes good and bad. The Christian belief is that these ideas have a common source in the form of a God-given conscience, the function of the human spirit which enables us to know right from wrong. The Bible says that faith in God is reasonable, disbelief is foolish, and judgment day is coming. It also teaches that man is without excuse regarding ignorance of God's existence; not only our conscience, but the resurrection and even creation itself provides proof:

He has fixed a day in which He will judge the world in righteousness through a Man whom He has appointed, having furnished proof to all men by raising Him from the dead. (Acts 17:31 NASB)

And that we may be delivered from unreasonable and wicked men: for all men have not faith. (2 Thes 3:2)

For what if some did not believe? Will their unbelief make the faithfulness of God without effect? Certainly not! Indeed, let God be true but every man a liar. (Ro 3:3-4a NKJV)

The fool hath said in his heart, There is no God. They are corrupt, they have done abominable works, there is none that doeth good. (Ps 14:1)

Because that which may be known of God is manifest in them; for God hath shewed it unto them. For the invisible things of him from the creation of the world are clearly seen, being understood by the things that are made, even his eternal power and Godhead; so that they are without excuse. (Ro 1:19-20)

Christians believe that what we do, what we think, and even what our motives are does matter because there will be a day of reckoning in the future, a day of perfect justice. That is why our Christian calling is to sound the warning of scripture that all men need salvation. It is left to the conscience and will of each hearer to believe the Gospel of Christ, or not to.

_____

_____

_____

20

"I don't need religion; I am close to God when I ____."
"I'm a very spiritual person."

> *There is a way which seemeth right unto a man, but the end thereof are the ways of death.* (Prov 14:12)

Christians believe that all men are sinners who are separated from God and in need of salvation from sin. The Bible states that a relationship with God is only through the Lord Jesus Christ, by faith in the Gospel message of 1 Corinthians 15:1-4. A belief held by many is that they do not need the Gospel because they have their "own way" to be close to God. According to the Bible, however, God has already revealed the way in which we can be close to Him.

If you believe that you have your own way to God, perhaps it is worth asking yourself how likely it is that the God of the universe will defer to the various "ways" conceived by man. If we assume there is a God, we can also probably assume that He has His own ideas about how things should be done. The Bible claims to be a credible authority for learning about God and why we need Him. But why should anyone believe the Bible?

Many books have been written which attest that the Bible is factual. The life, death, burial, and resurrection of Jesus Christ are well-documented events in ancient history, and the Bible has been the best-selling book for as long as there have been books to sell. Additionally, although many Christians suffer, are persecuted, and have every reason to abandon Jesus, the Christian faith has not been extinguished. These facts suggest that the Christian faith has more to recommend it than do other faith systems, and that the way to a relationship with God, as revealed in the Bible, may be worth considering. Perhaps there is some value in looking at teachings which have stood the test of time, rather than assuming that an idea in one's own mind is acceptable to God. If you value the idea of a spiritual relationship, we hope that you will look further into the one offered by the Gospel of Christ, found in 1 Corinthians 15:1-4.

21

"Christians are hypocrites. Why should I be held accountable for what I do, when that famous Christian did _____?!"

What then? are we better than they? No, in no wise: for we have before proved both Jews and Gentiles, that they are all under sin; As it is written, There is none righteous, no, not one... (Ro 3:9-10)

It is not uncommon for people to judge a group by the disobedience of a few of its members. Every few years, a Christian leader is in the news, attached to a scandal. Christians are human; at times we sin, make poor choices, and disregard the very thing we preach. We, as writers, make no excuse for any individual. In regard to the group, however, which is sullied by association, we offer some points to consider in regard to this objection.

Firstly, Christians are individuals, so claiming that all are hypocrites, for example, is simply not factual. Secondly, what some people do in disobedience to the faith is not the fault of God or the faith and, therefore, is not a reason to reject it. Thirdly, the Bible teaches that every person will one day face God with his sins, regardless of whether it appears as if he escaped the consequences of his actions for the present time. For these reasons, one need not discard Christianity because its followers are imperfect; everyone is imperfect. What matters in regard to the case for Christianity is not the failings of its adherents, but whether or not its judge is just. If God exists and the Bible is true, denying one's own need for a solution to sin while pointing to the sins of others does not remove anyone from God's final accounting for sin.

A fourth point may also strengthen Christianity's case against the charge of hypocrisy: the Bible teaches that Christians are held to a much higher standard in their earthly lives than are non-Christians:

> *For whom the Lord loveth he chasteneth, and scourgeth every son whom he receiveth. If ye endure chastening, God dealeth with you as with sons; for what son is he whom the father chasteneth not?* (Heb 12:6-7)

> *For the time is come that judgment must begin at the house of God: and if it first begin at us, what shall the end be of them that obey not the gospel of God? And if the righteous scarcely be saved, where shall the ungodly and the sinner appear?* (1 Pet 4:17-18)

The Bible is a large book rather than a leaflet for a reason; everybody needs much instruction and has much to learn. There is not a person alive who lives in perfect accordance with his own values, much less God's, so anyone can be deemed a hypocrite. Christians are forgiven, but they have no license to sin. Some will even face divine discipline for persistent sin (Heb 12:5-11), but on judgment day, they will not pay with their lives. Jesus already paid with His.

22

"I can believe what I want."

Absolutely, yes you can! The results, however, might not be what you would hope. Entrusting one's life to an idea which has little or no evidence or certainty is a gamble. The Bible has evidence that it is true, and it offers comfort and security regarding life after death. Trusting in unproven things is not the wisest course to take in life, let alone in eternity. The same God who allows you to do and believe what you like is also your Creator, who has readied for you a wonderful future if you will only believe the Gospel of Christ, found in 1 Corinthians 15:1-4.

> *Come now, and let us reason together, saith the LORD: though your sins be as scarlet, they shall be as white as snow; though they be red like crimson, they shall be as wool.* (Isa 1:18)

CHAPTER FIVE

HOW TO GET IT

Believe

For the message of the cross is foolishness to those who are perishing, but to us who are being saved it is the power of God. (1 Cor 1:18, NKJV)

According to the teachings of Christianity, to gain salvation from sin and its consequences, one must believe the Gospel of Christ, a message found in 1 Corinthians 15:1-4. Objections to the "how" of salvation commonly take the form of legalism, the observance of religious law in addition to faith, a topic covered in Chapter 3. But others deny the need for faith or equate Christianity with the faith claims of other religions. Whether replacing faith with religious observances or redefining biblical faith, those who promote such ideas share something in common; they all express faith in something, even if it is only in their own surmising. In this chapter, we ask you to consider the biblical teaching that nothing more than faith in the death, burial, and resurrection of Jesus Christ for the sins of the world is necessary to enter into a relationship with God.

23

"Jesus died for the sins of the world, so everyone is saved. They may not know Jesus, but He still died for their sins."
"All roads lead to heaven."

> *He that believeth on him is not condemned: but he that believeth not is condemned already, because he hath not believed in the name of the only begotten Son of God.*
> (Jn 3:18)

Salvation by faith alone is affirmed throughout the entire Bible. To exercise faith is to look away from oneself and trust God for deliverance from the penalty for sin. It simply means to believe God. Denying that faith is the condition for salvation can take a "Christian" or non-Christian form. In the Christian form, some "believe in Jesus" in such a way as to conclude that everyone has already been saved because of Him. A person who believes in this way may agree that Jesus is the Savior who died for the sins of the world and conclude that because all sins were paid on the cross, all people will be saved. The problem with this view is that it contradicts the Bible, which requires a *particular* belief about Jesus: that He died on a cross, was buried, and was resurrected for sins. In other words, the condition for salvation is to place one's faith in the Gospel message. The particulars of the Gospel are important because the Gospel itself says that it is the message "by which" we are saved. If one does not believe the message by which we are saved, then according to the Gospel, one is not saved. Jesus' death, burial, and resurrection is viewed by Christianity as a victory over sin and its consequence: death.

> "So when this corruptible shall have put on incorruption, and this mortal shall have put on immortality, then shall be brought to pass the saying that is written, Death is swallowed up in victory. O death, where is thy sting? O grave, where is thy victory? ... But thanks be to God, which giveth us the victory through our Lord Jesus Christ."
> (1 Cor 15:54-55, 57)

There is also a non-Christian version of denying the need for faith in the Gospel of Christ; it is the belief system known as Universalism. It teaches universal salvation, meaning that all mankind is saved, regardless of one's brand of religion. While it may seem to be a more kindly message to allow all mankind to enter heaven without condition, it creates another problem: the issue of justice.

The God of the Bible is a perfectly just God. He proclaims that all men are sinners and that all men are separated from His holy presence because of it. He does not determine the destiny of man, but offers man a choice: heaven or hell, communion or separateness, acceptance or rejection of His will. A belief system which denies the requirement of faith for salvation takes away the choice that God has given us all. It assumes that we all go to—and want to go to—the same place.

Faith in the Gospel requires one to recognize his sinfulness and his need of a savior from that sin. Only then can God lovingly apply forgiveness to it. Providing a perfect eternity to unrepentant sinners would not be just. Therefore, without the condition of belief, there can be no justice.

Belief in the Gospel of Christ is more than assenting to facts. In order to believe it, one must recognize one's own guilt before

God. God wishes for all to be saved; He created the Bible, and the church, and has called missionaries, pastors, evangelists, and every Christian man and woman to proclaim this message of forgiveness to all who will recognize their need for it. Yet it still belongs to the heart of each individual to accept the Gospel or to reject it.

___

___

___

24

"What about the people who haven't heard?" (aka "What about the guy in Bongo Bongo?")

For this is good and acceptable in the sight of God our Saviour; Who will have all men to be saved, and to come unto the knowledge of the truth. (1 Tim 2:3-4)

The objection that we affectionately call "the guy in Bongo Bongo" is based on an imaginary man who has never heard the Gospel. Among the many assumptions behind this objection to faith in the Gospel is the belief that there are people who have no awareness of Christianity and no way to hear the Gospel. If hearing the Gospel is not an option, it is further assumed that an alternative way of salvation is needed. In order to be just, God must accept whatever religious effort is made by "the guy in Bongo Bongo."

From the biblical perspective, man does as he wishes in rebellion against God, and yet he remains persistently religious. Christians believe that this is due to the fact that when the human spirit is not used in accordance with its function to commune with God, man seeks another means of fulfillment, such as through the practice of religious rituals. Perhaps because of the influence of The Theory of Evolution, additional assumptions are needed in order to support the "Bongo Bongo objection," such as the isolation, ignorance, and incapability of remote peoples.

Contrary to the notion that "primitive" peoples haven't "evolved," in actuality, remote societies have managed to survive, keeping themselves warm, fed, and sheltered. They have populated far-flung islands, made discoveries, and passed along survival skills for generations. They seem quite capable. Considering also that missionaries have been traveling and sharing information for two thousand years, we cannot assume that remote peoples have not heard the Gospel.

The biblical record shows that man has been man all along, with intelligence, skills, and abilities given by God. The "Bongo Bongo objection" is ultimately an attack on God's character, accusing Him of leaving people with no way to be saved. God, however, desires for all to be saved, because God is love (1 Jn 4:8b). The existence of false religion does not mean that God has left some people with no way to find the truth, nor does it necessitate that God contradict His word and allow alternative ways of salvation. Bibles, churches, missionaries, and believers are everywhere. We can trust God to get the truth of how to be saved to those who want to know Him.

If any man will do his will, he shall know of the doctrine…
(Jn 7:17a)

And ye shall seek me, and find me, when ye shall search for me with all your heart. (Jer 29:13)

Because that which may be known of God is manifest in them; for God hath shewed it unto them. For the invisible things of him from the creation of the world are clearly seen, being understood by the things that are made, even his eternal power and Godhead; so that they are without excuse... (Ro 1:19-20)

25

"Faith in the Christian Gospel cannot be the only way to heaven. What about all the other religions?" "Different religions; same god."

Jesus saith unto him, I am the way, the truth, and the life: no man cometh unto the Father, but by me. (Jn 14:6)

Some objections to faith in the Gospel of Christ take issue with its exclusivity. With a custom-designed way of salvation for everyone, this "politically correct" view of religion is defeated by the fact that every religious belief cannot be true. With vastly different ideas about "god" as well as different teachings and objectives, other religions contradict each other and lack evidence that their claims are factual. Christianity is unique and shares nothing in common with the religions of the world.

Objecting to the exclusivity of the Gospel message—that there is no other way of salvation than through faith in Jesus Christ as Savior—is not solved by turning to other religions. Most of them make exclusive claims as well. Denying Christianity because of its exclusivity eliminates every religion with an exclusive claim.

There is another problem with reasoning that there may be a way of salvation while denying that Christianity is that way. If Jesus is not the way of salvation, and a religion other than Christianity was "the one true faith," how would anyone know it? It would be an insurmountable problem to objectively evaluate all of the world's belief systems, evenly scoring each by its merits, historical accuracy, evidence, logic, and reasonableness in order to know what to believe. Many religions have been lost to history. What if one of those was the "real" one? We, the authors, conclude that only God could show us His plan, as well as provide proof of it. We also believe that He has done so. We are convinced that we do not need to scour the earth to find the truth of salvation, nor settle for the conundrum of competing claims. The true God settled the question by revealing Himself to us. He stepped into time and changed the world forever. He provided a book that cannot be disproven and He changed the heart of man.

Christianity is a "religion" like no other, not only because of the miraculous life, death, burial, and resurrection of Jesus, but also because it stands alone in declaring that man cannot save himself. The world religions cannot guarantee anything; they cannot prove anything, and they cannot save. From the Christian perspective, our God, just as a loving father would, took it upon Himself to save us, promising each believer an eternity which is forever safe with Him.

He saw that there was no man, And wondered that there was no intercessor; Therefore His own arm brought salvation for Him; And His own righteousness, it sustained Him.
(Isa 59:16 NKJV)

___

___

___

26

"So you're saying no Hindus or Muslims or Buddhists are saved?"
"So you're saying my grandma is in hell?"
"So your belief is right and everybody else is wrong?!"

No man can come to me, except the Father which hath sent me draw him: and I will raise him up at the last day.
(Jn 6:44)

Sometimes an objection to the Christian faith is a reaction to the realization that if the Gospel of Christ is true, it precludes another way of salvation. You may ask yourself, "How can I accept the Gospel, knowing what it means for others I care about?" You may know people who have already passed on, who did not believe the Gospel as far as you know. This is understandably difficult to reconcile, especially if you think that the Gospel may have merit. It may seem that Christians are acting as know-it-alls, pronouncing the eternal destiny of others. The issue, however, is not about Christian people or anyone else; it is about what the Bible teaches regarding how one is saved.

It may be of some comfort to learn more about the character of God as described in the Bible. God the Son created us and died to save us. Working through human authors, He has written a large book of verifiable information about Himself and about salvation. He has sent ministers and missionaries all over the world, spreading the good news of salvation from sin. If any person wants to know how to be saved, God does not keep the truth hidden; He is drawing all men to Himself through the preaching of the Gospel. Another point to consider is that in our country especially, it is unlikely that someone would get through life without ever hearing the Gospel, attending church, or having access to a Bible. No person who wants to know God will be prevented.

Ultimately, the issue of salvation is not location, culture, or the religion of one's family, but whether or not a person accepts the Bible as the authority regarding salvation. The Gospel message of eternal salvation by faith alone can elicit strong emotion. Many of us know others who believe in a different religious system. We can only point you to the biblical record of the love and justice of God and encourage you to consider the Gospel of Christ, found in 1 Corinthians 15:1-4.

27

"I believe in me."
"I have my own beliefs."
"You have your way; I have mine."
"Let's agree to disagree."
"All religions are equal; let's co-exist."

> *The next day John seeth Jesus coming unto him, and saith, Behold the Lamb of God, which taketh away the sin of the world.* (Jn 1:29)

Some of you who read this book may not have any particular objection to the Gospel of Christ. You aren't offended or threatened by it because you consider religion a personal choice. You are fine with what others choose to believe or practice and you are not concerned about eternity. You may consider yourself to have "faith" in everything or in nothing, feeling more apathy than hostility toward religion. Perhaps you find the Christian persistence to promote Jesus to be perplexing, pointless, or problematic.

Although the "let's get along" idea is popular and seems reasonable, it asserts an idea about Christianity which is false. From the Christian perspective, we are not refusing to "get along" or to "co-exist" by sharing the Gospel; we are testifying to the truth. We desire that others be saved so they may know the joy, love, peace, and hope that salvation from sin provides. If deliverance from sin is not a concern for you, please ask yourself if you have ever done something that you would classify as a sin. Did you ever disobey your parents, tell a lie, or break a traffic law, for example? We all know that wrongs done in this world usually have consequences; is it reasonable then to believe that God also has consequences for sin? If accountability for having sinned seems like a possibility, or if an afterlife exists, the Bible's solution may be worth considering. Accountability for sin is part of what gives life here its meaningfulness; if there is no accountability in the future, how people behave does not matter very much.

As for other religions, none of them have a solution to the problem of sin. The best they can offer is good works in this life to appease their deity, none of which remove the guilt of having sinned against God. They cannot prove the claims of their respective religious systems. If there is a creator and an existence beyond this world, being right about how to gain salvation is of everlasting significance. Tolerance, acceptance, and belief in oneself are admirable principles and are useful for some things, but it is not wise to go your own way when you don't know where you are going. That is why Christians continue to promote the death, burial, and resurrection of God the Son as payment for the sins of the world. We are convinced that it is the truth which enables all who trust in it to enter into an eternal relationship with God.

_____

_____

_____

28

"I don't need to understand the Bible; I take it by faith."
"Faith is a blind leap, a leap in the dark."
"I hope I make it."

> *Even as Abraham believed God, and it was accounted to him for righteousness.* (Gal 3:6)

Some objections to faith as the way of salvation are not actually to faith per se, but are due to a faulty definition of faith. Although a person may claim to have faith, if he describes his understanding of faith as a wish, not as a surety, it is not faith. Faith must be directed at an object, such as toward the good character of God or a promise made by Him. If faith is not in something which is sure, it is merely wishful thinking. Faith in the Gospel of Christ is a conviction of mind regarding how one is saved; The death, burial, and resurrection of Jesus Christ in payment for the sins of the world is the object of faith for salvation, according to Christian belief.

The Bible defines faith as being "fully persuaded" that the facts being presented are true:

> *And being fully persuaded that, what He had promised, He was also able to perform.* (Ro 4:21)

> *These all died in faith, not having received the promises, but having seen them afar off, and were persuaded of them, and embraced them, and confessed that they were strangers and pilgrims on the earth.* (Heb 11:13)

> *Knowing therefore the terror of the Lord, we persuade men; but we are made manifest unto God; and I trust also are made manifest in your consciences.* (2 Cor 5:11)

The Bible also teaches us that faith has substance and evidence:

Now faith is the substance of things hoped for, the evidence of things not seen. (Heb 11:1)

Each of us is to believe the good news of salvation because it is reasonable and true:

And he reasoned in the synagogue every Sabbath, and persuaded the Jew and the Greeks. (Acts 18:4; see also Acts 19:8, 28:23)

And that we may be delivered from unreasonable and wicked men: for all men have not faith. (2 Thes 3:2)

Unfortunately, 19th century German philosophy seeped into some Christian theology, introducing the erroneous idea that faith is a "leap." Such a teaching is a perversion of biblical faith and is, in fact, the opposite of faith. The salvation message is not, "Maybe you'll get to heaven, so cross your fingers." Salvation is presented as a surety for those who believe the Gospel. Christians find the truthfulness of the Bible to be evident; therefore, its call to know God by reading His word contradicts the idea of being in the dark. It is left to each person who wishes to know the teachings of the Bible to look into it further and come to his own conviction as to whether faith in the Gospel is really the way by which one is saved.

_____

_____

_____

29

"I don't know."
"Nobody can know."

> *These things have I written unto you that believe on the name of the Son of God; that ye may know that ye have eternal life, and that ye may believe on the name of the Son of God.*
> (1 Jn 5:13)

The Bible is unique among religious writings. It is more than a book of doctrine; it is the history book of a people, the ancient nation of Israel. A nation's historical records are not as easy to dismiss as are the clearly mythological writings of some religions, for example. The thousands of volumes written about the Bible, ranging from law to archeology, add further doubt to the idea that the Bible's God cannot be known.

Because faith must be in something which can be known and trusted, an objection to faith for salvation may be an admission that you personally do not know what is true, perhaps because you have not studied the matter. This position is known as agnosticism. Others take this further, however, and refute the absolute claim of the Bible to be the word of God by making another absolute claim, which is that truth cannot be known by anyone. There is a problem with the latter reasoning: if one cannot know that something is true, then neither can one know it is not true. Therefore, it could be true. We assert that the Bible is the only religious book that *can* be proven true.

The Bible is a very large book containing a large amount of information, much of it plainly factual, such as Israel's national history. The Bible claims to be much more, however; it claims to be

God's revelation of Himself. The Apostle Paul explains in Romans Chapters 1 and 2 that God's existence has been made obvious through the intricacies of creation and the existence of the human conscience: A created thing needs a creator, and a conscience requires a judge. The God of the Bible says that He is those things, and many more, such as a father, a comforter, and a savior.

The Christian faith is founded on the content of the Bible; without the assurance that it can be known and understood, what would we have? Christians are convinced that we can know and have assurance of our eternal destiny. Things that are not known to be true can only be wished for, and we believe the Bible offers much more than that. The Bible may be worth exploring; you may find that your faith in it grows as you study it more.

_____

_____

_____

30

"I already believe in God; I don't need all those details."
"You're being picky. Just believe in Jesus."

> *For if he that cometh preacheth another Jesus, whom we have not preached, or if ye receive another spirit, which ye have not received, or another gospel, which ye have not accepted, ye might well bear with him. (2 Cor 11:4)*

Sometimes an objection to faith in the Gospel is characterized by an apparent aversion to defining terminology. Christians who stand up for an accurate Gospel are sometimes accused of being picky or "legalistic," but the Gospel itself is a message, and a message is either transmitted accurately or inaccurately. To deny this is to put oneself in the odd position of defending inaccuracy.

Faith in the Gospel of Christ is not a general, nebulous belief, such as a belief in some "higher power" with no particular traits. Because salvation is by faith, one's faith must be placed in the correct object, namely Jesus Christ and His payment for sin. Therefore, one cannot believe the Gospel without knowing its elements.

We, as authors, believe it is not "picky" to handle God's word carefully and share the Gospel accurately. The many objections within this book show that the Gospel can be misunderstood in a startling number of ways. A person who claims that it is good enough to "just believe in Jesus" needs to look to the Bible as the authority and its explanation of who Jesus is, what He did, and why. The object of saving faith is the Jesus of the Bible, not a generic "Jesus." Genuine faith in the Gospel of Christ is a belief in the particulars of its saving message. Although it is up to each person to accept or reject the Gospel, Christianity is defined by its message and by nothing else.

31

"I was born a _____, and I'll die a _____."
"There are so many denominations; how do I know yours is right?"

> *There is neither Jew nor Greek, there is neither bond nor free, there is neither male nor female: for ye are all one in Christ Jesus.* (Gal 3:28)

Sometimes hearing the Gospel message highlights the differences between Christian denominations. There are many churches which would disagree with the simple message that faith in the death, burial, and resurrection of Jesus Christ for sin is sufficient to deliver a person from the eternal consequences of sin. You may have heard a salvation message presented before now and wondered if what you were hearing was what the Bible said, or if it was from the denomination of the person sharing it. The issue of denominations had already begun in a rudimentary way during the ministry of the Apostle Paul, who admonished the church at Corinth for dividing and following individuals:

> *"Now I beseech you, brethren, by the name of our Lord Jesus Christ, that ye all speak the same thing, and that there be no divisions among you; but that ye be perfectly joined together in the same mind and in the same judgment. For it hath been declared unto me of you, my brethren, by them which are of the house of Chloe, that there are contentions among you. Now this I say, that every one of you saith, I am of Paul; and I of Apollos; and I of Cephas; and I of Christ. Is Christ divided? was Paul crucified for you? or were ye baptized in the name of Paul?"* (1 Cor 1:10-13)

One of the reasons that this book has so many Bible verses is so that readers can easily compare the objections in it with what the Bible says. Because Christian salvation is by faith in a biblical message, each reader must be persuaded in his own mind that the Gospel message is true. Christianity is the one faith that nobody is born into; they are only re-born into it. The Christian birth results from a change of mind and from nothing else; no baby is born knowing the Gospel message. For this reason, it is important that you ask yourself if you are trusting in being born into a "Christian family" or into a particular Christian denomination rather than trusting the Gospel. A person is born again when he first hears the Gospel and believes, or if he has heard it before, when he changes his mind and trusts it for salvation.

The Bible is the Christian's source of authority, and it teaches that salvation is by faith, not by membership in any particular group or organization. If elements within the Gospel of Christ suggest to you that your church or denomination is in disagreement with the message of 1 Corinthians 15:1-4, perhaps your pastor is best suited to explain it.

God does not recognize denominations; according to the Bible, He recognizes those who believe Him, namely, His message of salvation, the Gospel of Christ. Many denominations believe the same fundamentals of the faith. They may have small differences or large ones, but for the purpose of this book, the issue of denominations is whether the differences between them affect one's salvation.

32

"I'm a Christian, but I don't believe in that 'born-again' stuff."

Being born again, not of corruptible seed, but of incorruptible, by the word of God, which liveth and abideth for ever. (1 Pet 1:23)

Some people do not have a positive view of the teaching known as being "born again." Unfortunately, the term has been associated with some unbiblical religious ideas. An objection to the biblical concept of being born again is sometimes simply a misunderstanding of terminology. In other cases it is a denial of what the term "born again" represents. According to the Bible, faith in the Gospel results in a spiritual birth. It refers to a reversal of man's condition of being separated from God (spiritually dead) due to sin. Not everybody is familiar with the teachings of the new birth, but it is mentioned several times in scripture. More information about the spiritual birth can be found in Chapter One.

Jesus answered and said unto him, Verily, verily, I say unto thee, Except a man be born again, he cannot see the kingdom of God... Marvel not that I said unto thee, Ye must be born again. (Jn 3:3, 7)

Blessed be the God and Father of our Lord Jesus Christ, who according to His great mercy has caused us to be born again to a living hope through the resurrection of Jesus Christ from the dead... (1 Pet 1:3 NASB)

33

"You have to repent."
"You need to turn from sin."
"Faith alone is 'easy-believism.'"

Of his own will begat he us with the word of truth... (Jas 1:18a)

Whosoever believeth that Jesus is the Christ is born of God... (1 Jn 5:1a)

Some objections to the teaching of faith alone for salvation amount to a difference in the use of words and their definitions, such as in the disagreements among some Christians regarding the word "repent." We, as writers, believe that the concept of repentance is imbedded within the meaning of saving faith; it is a change of mind from what was believed before, to agreement with the Gospel message. Some believe, however, that repentance is a change of behavior, describing it as "turning from sin." This definition implies a moral reform, which is contrary to gracious salvation.

The main problem with adding to the Gospel a promise of future behavioral improvement is that salvation is a gift which is graciously given and excludes any kind of human effort. Therefore, the Gospel of Christ cannot include a performance standard. Additionally, no person can promise what his future behavior will be. He may have good intentions, but because his future actions cannot be guaranteed, they cannot be part of salvation. Adding a behavioral condition to salvation would make one's status with God unknown and unknowable. Furthermore, the idea that one must "turn from sin" to be saved is impossible. If any person must enumerate his sins and then turn from them to get saved, he would never get saved nor would anyone. According to the Bible, an unsaved person is spiritually dead; he cannot turn from sin nor obey the command to live according to God's will. Even if "turning from sin" is defined only as a mental determination to obey God, it still adds a requirement that is not in the Gospel of Christ. Although a general awareness of being separated from God because of sin is implied by the fact that we need a savior, God does not require anyone to make a promise of future behavior in order to be saved.

Christian salvation is not "cleaning up your act," "turning over a new leaf," or "determining to forsake sin." Salvation is a spiritual birth resulting from believing the contents of a message which provide spiritual illumination. One of the sources of confusion regarding salvation is the misapplication of verses which explain Christian maturity. Recognizing sin and allowing the Holy Spirit to empower a God-honoring Christian life is part of maturity *after* one is saved. It is not a condition to be saved. Salvation from the penalty of sin is graciously given when one exercises faith in the Gospel.

Another source for this objection is in regard to the sufficiency of grace through faith for salvation, a topic which is covered in Chapter 3. Convinced that there is something more to salvation than just believing a message, some may call salvation by faith alone "easy-believism." Such people might have difficulty believing that the Gospel is so simple and pure. But it has to be pure; it cannot be tainted with the works of a sinner. The phrase "by which also ye are saved," found in the Apostle Paul's Gospel presentation could not be plainer; he meant that its elements are sufficient to save.

34

"If you think you can just believe on your own, that's decisional regeneration—you think you saved yourself with your decision."
"We are too depraved by sin to believe."
"I was chosen."

> *So then faith cometh by hearing, and hearing by the word of God.* (Ro 10:17)

Not everyone who objects to the Gospel has an objection to the elements within it. Some instead disagree about how one becomes a Christian. You may have been taught that man is incapable of responding to the Gospel or exercising saving faith in the Gospel message. Because the Bible calls us to hear and believe, our view as writers is that man *can* respond in faith. We also believe that there is a difference between "deciding" and "believing." We do not agree that our ability to comprehend the call to believe is the equivalent of saving oneself through a decision. By defining faith as the Bible does—as being persuaded of facts—we are not "deciding" to believe, but have been convinced by God's word and the Holy Spirit that the Gospel of Christ is true.

> *For what saith the scripture? Abraham believed God, and it was counted unto him for righteousness. …He staggered not at the promise of God through unbelief; but was strong in faith, giving glory to God; And being fully persuaded that, what he had promised, he was able also to perform. And therefore it was imputed to him for righteousness.* (Ro 4:3, 20-22)

Another variation of this objection is that the exercise of faith amounts to "doing something" to get saved. This view considers faith itself to be a work. When we believe, however, we are not "doing" anything, because the Bible specifically excludes faith as a work. It, in fact, contrasts faith and work as opposites:

> But to him that **worketh not, but believeth** on him that justifieth the ungodly, his faith is counted for righteousness. (Ro 4:5)

Faith in the Gospel of Christ is not a work done by me, but the recognition that somebody else did something for me, namely that Jesus died on the cross to pay for my sins. We refer you again to the Gospel itself which calls us to believe. It is detailed in Chapter One.

35

"Yes I'm saved...as long as...." (...I don't turn my back on Jesus ...I don't sin too much ...I don't commit the unpardonable sin ...I don't fall away ...I keep believing ...I repent when I sin.)

> Now unto him that is able to keep you from falling, and to present you faultless before the presence of his glory with exceeding joy... (Jude 1:24)

This objection to faith for salvation is a "what-if" type of objection to faith; it is an outcome-based belief for which faith is not the determining factor of salvation. Salvation is secure only "if" one avoids some sins, limits others, or quickly repents afterward.

Rejecting faith alone for salvation is ultimately a form of legalism, and is covered in Chapter Three. In this view, that which makes one a Christian or keeps one a Christian is not Jesus, but oneself. A certain sin I commit may render Christ's payment for sin ineffective for my salvation.

A "what-if" objection is not compatible with Christianity because the Bible teaches that Christ paid for the sins of the world and that His provision is available to any who will accept it by faith. There is no security in an outcome-based system because it is essentially a maintenance plan to "stay saved," with no assurance of one's eternal destiny. If our sins are not fully paid, we are not actually saved from anything. If one who has believed the Gospel is still at risk of hell, the entire concept of being "saved" is meaningless.

A further problem with the belief in some unpardonable sin or cancellation of salvation is that it not only makes the sacrifice of Christ foolish, but also makes the Father's plan to make Jesus a sacrifice an unjust one. God knows all; why would He send the Son to die for a salvation that would not be effective to save? Why would the Son bother to participate in this fruitless effort? Is the Bible mistaken when it declares the believer safe with the Holy Spirit's irreversible seal? Is God taunting us with a half-hearted effort to save us? These are questions that may help clarify the need for salvation to be secured without the uncertainty created by human participation.

In some cases, this objection arises because a person has taken for himself a warning to the nation of Israel. Jesus warned the Jews that they would be set aside if they called the Holy Spirit a liar, as they had already done to the Father and were about to do to Jesus

(Mk 3:28-29). Another cause of this objection is due to confusing God's parental discipline of the believer with the final judgment of the unsaved. Bible verses which relate to the Christian's loss of rewards are misunderstood to mean a loss of one's saved status. The Bible, however, teaches that believers are "sealed unto the day of redemption" by the Holy Spirit, Himself, and we are, therefore, secure. Turning one's back on Jesus is just another sin for which He has fully paid.

> Now he which stablisheth us with you in Christ, and hath anointed us, is God; Who hath also sealed us, and given the earnest of the Spirit in our hearts. (2 Cor 1:21-22)
>
> In whom ye also trusted, after that ye heard the word of truth, the gospel of your salvation: in whom also after that ye believed, ye were sealed with that holy Spirit of promise… (Eph 1:13)
>
> And grieve not the holy Spirit of God, whereby ye are sealed unto the day of redemption. (Eph 4:30)

The Bible teaches that salvation from sin is by grace through faith. Christians believe that the grace that saves us must also keep us, or else what Jesus provided on the cross cannot be considered salvation at all.

36

"Yes I'm saved. I...." (...prayed the sinner's prayer ...was baptized ...was confirmed ...went forward at an altar call ...asked Jesus into my heart ...gave my life to Jesus ...made a decision for Christ ...made Jesus the Lord of my life.)

> *Forasmuch as ye know that ye were not redeemed with corruptible things, as silver and gold, from your vain conversation received by tradition from your fathers; But with the precious blood of Christ, as of a lamb without blemish and without spot: Who verily was foreordained before the foundation of the world, but was manifest in these last times for you, Who by him do believe in God, that raised him up from the dead, and gave him glory; that your faith and hope might be in God.* (1 Pet 1:18-21)

Sometimes a disagreement about faith for salvation is not an objection, but a blending of faith with a church activity or ceremony which accompanied faith. Examples of this may include things such as "asking Jesus into your heart," praying the "sinner's prayer," responding to an altar call, being dipped into water or having it poured or sprinkled, completing church classes and making a public declaration, or some similar agreement or assent to biblical facts. Doing such things may or may not accompany faith in the Gospel. They are not, however, the equivalent of believing the content of the Gospel of Christ. The actions listed in this objection and other similar things need to be distinguished from salvation in order to provide a clear understanding of the saving message. 1 Corinthians 15:1-4 proclaims it is the message "by which" we are saved, and does not contain any additions such as those listed.

Similarly, popular Christian phrases, such as "following Jesus" or "turning your life over to Jesus," are treated as if they are the equivalent of the Gospel of Christ. But such things do not convey the meaning of the Gospel or provide the object of faith for salvation. You may be someone who agreed to "follow Jesus," for example, without understanding that salvation is by grace through faith in the elements contained in 1 Corinthians 15:1-4. Short-cut phrases without definitions are certainly not intended to obscure the Gospel, but they can and do.

If you are not sure that you correctly understand the Gospel, you may wish to ask yourself questions such as: Do I think that the prayer I prayed resulted in my salvation? Do I think I would be saved had I not been baptized with water? Do I understand the elements of the death, burial, and resurrection of Jesus and its purpose, or did I simply agree when asked about it?

Further clarification comes from knowing that sinful human beings have nothing to offer Almighty God. The Gospel asks us to accept what *He* did. In faith, we look away from our own perceived goodness and recognize the perfect sacrificial work of another. No works done, no goodness maintained, no sin repented of, or prayer sincerely prayed can save. According to the Bible, only Jesus saves, and He does so through the Gospel message, by faith.

_____

_____

_____

CHAPTER SIX
WHERE TO FIND IT

The Bible

...it is written...

At least eighty verses in the Bible include the phrase, "it is written." God continually directs Bible readers to His written word. An objection about the Bible is an objection to the Gospel's source of authority. Christians believe that without the record of the Bible, mankind has no authoritative source of information about God.

The Bible claims to be the record of God's message to mankind. In comparing this written record with his miraculous experiences, the Apostle Peter calls the scripture "a more sure word of prophecy," preserving God's message throughout time (2 Pet 1:19). The Apostle John warns that those who "believeth not the record that God gave of his Son" are calling God a liar (1 Jn 5:10b).

Trusting the Bible matters to the Christian faith, since it contains the message of salvation. Anyone who is willing to consider the evidence of the Bible's trustworthiness and reliability as a source of information has a good foundation for faith in the Gospel of Christ, found in 1 Corinthians 15:1-4.

37

"The Bible is full of errors and contradictions."
"It couldn't possibly be the same Bible after 2000 years."
"It has been changed by the translators."
"There is no way that _____ happened."

> *But the word of the Lord endureth for ever. And this is the word which by the gospel is preached unto you.* (1 Pet 1:25)

It is a foundation of Christianity that the Bible contains no mistakes or contradictions. The original writings were perfect, and the copies passed down are reliable. The small variations among the thousands of copied manuscripts do not change its teachings. Of course, few of us read the Bible in its original language; therefore, some people object to the trustworthiness of the translation process. While few Christians are able to address the complexities of the meticulous science of translation, neither are most of those who deny the Bible's accuracy language experts who can support their objections. The bottom line is that the God who created the universe is definitely able to preserve His book.

The integrity of the Bible, its supernatural claims, and its many miracles may be difficult to believe, but the Gospel does not direct its readers to those debates. It simply asks us to acknowledge both our sinfulness and our need of righteousness to stand before a holy God. If you wish to learn more about the Bible as a trustworthy historical record, many books have been written to defend its authority and reliability. If you can in a general way consider the Bible to be worthy of consideration, you may consider its offer of eternity to be worthy as well.

> *You performed signs and wonders in Egypt and have continued them to this day, in Israel and among all mankind, and have gained the renown that is still yours.* (Jer 32:20 NIV)

38
"It's a good book, but it's not inspired."
"It was written by men."

All scripture is given by inspiration of God…" (2 Tim 3:16a)

The Bible is a very old book. Its newest entries are nearly 2000 years old. Because of its antiquity, some question how we can be certain of its authorship. Isn't the claim that God wrote it just Christian mythology? The objection to the Bible's claim of divine authorship overlooks the fact that the very men who put their name to the letters they wrote are the ones giving credit to God for their writings. They themselves did not believe that the authorship of scripture consisted of men alone, but believed that they were inspired by God to write.

As Christian authors, we find it humorous that many people are convinced that there is a psychic connection between thinking about a friend and then receiving a call from him, but would object to the idea that God could inspire a person to write. To deny the divine origin of the Bible is to put oneself in the role of Bible expert. But true experts, even many who set out to discredit the Bible, find its claims convincing. Each person has the choice to decide for himself if he believes the record of scripture or if he is at least interested enough to learn more about the evidence of its supernatural character. The doctrine of the inspiration of scripture is not a matter of opinion to the Christian, but is a foundation of Christianity:

> *For the prophecy came not in old time by the will of man: but holy men of God spake as they were moved by the Holy Ghost.* (2 Pet 1:21)

We hope this brief chapter about the importance of the Bible encourages you to learn more about it.

39

"That's your opinion; this is what it means to me." "You can make the Bible mean anything you want."

> *Knowing this first, that no prophecy of the scripture is of any private interpretation.* (2 Pet 1:20)

There are those who consider the Bible to be a nice inspirational book, but believe its contents are only a matter of opinion. Some passages may hold personal meaning but have no broader significance. Taking this objection even further, some say that the Bible's contents can mean anything.

Of course, we all know that words have meaning, and that they cannot mean anything. If it were not so, people would not be able to communicate with each other. For example, a cookbook recipe cannot mean anything, nor can a set of assembly instructions, a grocery list, or a utility bill. While it is true that words can have multiple meanings, even those are narrowed by the immediate context. In the case of the Bible, the meanings of its verses are made even more precise by historical context. If you hold this objection, you may want to select a passage of scripture and try to make it mean anything. You will find that there is little room for variation in its interpretation.

In some cases, this objection is related to the differences among various Christian denominations. As Christian witnesses ourselves, we have encountered those who are distressed by the existence of so many kinds of churches and the differences between them. The fact that Christians disagree on the finer points of the faith, however, is a far cry from being able to make the Bible mean anything. Any person could spend a lifetime studying the contents of the Bible, and many have. But in regard to salvation, it is the death, burial, and resurrection of Jesus Christ for sins that saves, and on that point, Christians agree.

40

"I Just Don't Believe It."

In whom the god of this world hath blinded the minds of them which believe not, lest the light of the glorious gospel of Christ, who is the image of God, should shine unto them. (2 Cor 4:4)

You may be a person who, when presented with the Gospel, just said, "No." Whether one is objecting to the historical facts of the Gospel, its authorship, its authority, or is simply disinterested, many people do not care to even formulate an objection. In this book, we have attempted to meet each objector at his own point of belief or disbelief. We were once there too.

As Christians, we believe the Bible, which says that the Lord, in His boundless longsuffering and mercy, wants every person to know Him and to be saved from sin. It also says that He protects the right of every person to reject the Gospel; no one will be forced into a relationship with Him or into heaven. If this describes you, please know that if you become willing to trust the source of the Gospel and to hear its message, your Creator will be patiently waiting.

CONCLUSION

WHAT THE GOSPEL ISN'T

And the LORD passed by before him, and proclaimed, The LORD, The LORD God, merciful and gracious, longsuffering, and abundant in goodness and truth… (Ex 34:6)

The Gospel is a lot to take in; eternity is a lot to think about. You may not know what you believe because you have never considered many of these matters before. Time is often required to process the new information and formulate questions. New information must be compared with former beliefs and assumptions, and choices must be made regarding ideas which have now been called into question.

Because we, the authors, were both raised in church-connected homes, we both called ourselves Christians long before we actually believed the Gospel. One thing that helped both of us recognize the saving message was to learn what it was *not*.

The Gospel of Christ is not a formula or "magic words" that one can say to be saved. It is not a prayer, a decision, or a request. It is not a calling out for something or a coming forward for something. It is not turning from sin, nor a promise to sin less in the future.

Neither is God's word a secondary source to confirm a sign or an experience. A person who imagines that he has become a believer because he has witnessed a miracle, for example, has only become a believer in the miracle.

The Gospel of Christ, found in 1 Corinthians 15:1-4, is a particular message which we are to believe in order to receive the gift of salvation. It is nothing more and nothing less. The Gospel is the death, burial, and resurrection of Jesus Christ, for the sins of the world, and according to the scriptures, attained by faith alone through the power of God's grace.

We find it comforting that God wants us to know Him because of His love for us, and that He wants us to do things His way because of His desire to protect us. The Bible teaches that the meaning of life is to know Him. We are now trying to learn all that He has already done for us, so that we can enjoy His kind provision for those who believe Him. We hope that you will soon be doing the same.

–Preston and Kelly

> *...and I count all things but loss for the excellency of the knowledge of Christ Jesus my Lord: for whom I have suffered the loss of all things, and do count them but dung, that I may win Christ, And be found in him, not having mine own righteousness, which is of the law, but that which is through the faith of Christ, the righteousness which is of God by faith: That I may know him, and the power of his resurrection, and the fellowship of his sufferings, being made conformable unto his death;* (Phil 3:8-10)

APPENDIX

INDEX OF OBJECTIONS

Objections to who He is
1. Jesus isn't God. 26
2. God is not a trinity. 30
3. The Bible has two different Gods. 34
4. God wouldn't send anyone to hell. 37
5. I reject a God who allows suffering. 40
6. I believe in a god of my own understanding.. 44

Objections to what He did
7. He didn't die for everyone's sins. 51
8. I need to do my share. 55
9. The Law is needed also. 57
10. I don't need it; I'm a good person. 64
11. I am a Christian; I go to church, live a Christian life, etc. . . 66
12. My good deeds outweigh my bad deeds. 67
13. I have my own beliefs. 69

Objections to why I need it
14. Religion is for other people. 74
15. My lifestyle is not a sin; God made me this way.. 79
16. I make mistakes, but I wouldn't call myself a sinner. 82
17. I'll believe later. 83

18. I am a Christian; I just don't believe what the Bible says
    about _____............................... 84
19. There is nothing after death. 86
20. I don't need religion; I am very spiritual................ 89
21. Christians are hypocrites.............................. 90
22. I can believe what I want............................. 92

Objections to how to get it

23. All roads lead to heaven; everybody is saved. 94
24. What about the guy who hasn't heard? 96
25. This can't be the only way. 98
26. You're right and everybody else is wrong?.............. 100
27. All religions are the same; let's co-exist................ 102
28. Faith is a blind leap.................................. 104
29. Nobody can know................................... 106
30. Just believe in (generic) Jesus; details are not necessary... 107
31. I was born a _____; I will die a _____.......... 109
32. I am a Christian; I just don't believe in being born again... 111
33. That's "easy-believism;" you need to repent and turn
    from sin. 112
34. That's decisional regeneration; we're too depraved to believe. . 114
35. Yes, I'm saved, as long as I don't _____............ 115
36. I'm already saved because I was baptized, prayed, went
    forward at an altar call, etc. 118

Objections to where to find it

37. The Bible is full of errors; it was changed in translation... 122
38. The Bible is not inspired; it was written by men. 123
39. The Bible's meaning is opinion; you can make it mean
    anything you want. 124
40. I just don't believe the Bible............................ 126

ABOUT THE AUTHORS

Preston Condra, M.Div., graduated from Oklahoma Baptist University and Southwestern Baptist Theological Seminary. He has been preaching, teaching, lecturing, writing, and appearing on broadcasts for more than twenty-five years. His wife Kelly, M.S.Ed., has been teaching and speaking throughout her career. Together, they founded Sufficient Word Ministries and have authored many books.

www.sufficientword.com